BEADING WITH PEARLS

BEADING WITH PEARLS

Beautiful Jewelry, Simple Techniques

Edited by Jean Campbell

LARK BOOKS
A Division of Sterling Publishing Co., Inc.
New York / London

Senior Editor
Valerie Van Arsdale Shrader

Production Editor
Nathalie Mornu

Art Director
Stacey Budge

Cover Designer
Cindy LaBreacht

Illustrators
J'aime Allene
Bonnie Brooks

Photographer
Stewart O'Shields

Library of Congress Cataloging-in-Publication Data

Beading with pearls / edited by Jean Campell. -- 1st ed.
     p. cm.
Includes index.
ISBN-13: 978-1-60059-037-5 (hc-plc with jacket : alk. paper)
ISBN-10: 1-60059-037-3 (hc-plc with jacket : alk. paper)
1. Beadwork. 2. Jewelry making. 3. Pearls. I. Campell, Jean.
TT860.B333965 2008
745.594'2--dc22

                              2007026947

10 9 8 7 6 5 4 3 2 1

First Edition

Published by Lark Books, A Division of
Sterling Publishing Co., Inc.
387 Park Avenue South, New York, NY 10016

Text © 2008, Lark Books
Photography © 2008, Lark Books unless otherwise specified
Illustrations © 2008, Lark Books unless otherwise specified

Distributed in Canada by Sterling Publishing,
c/o Canadian Manda Group, 165 Dufferin Street
Toronto, Ontario, Canada M6K 3H6

Distributed in the United Kingdom by GMC Distribution Services,
Castle Place, 166 High Street, Lewes, East Sussex, England BN7 1XU

Distributed in Australia by Capricorn Link (Australia) Pty Ltd.,
P.O. Box 704, Windsor, NSW 2756 Australia

The written instructions, photographs, designs, patterns, and
projects in this volume are intended for the personal use of the
reader and may be reproduced for that purpose only. Any other use,
especially commercial use, is forbidden under law without written
permission of the copyright holder.

Every effort has been made to ensure that all the information in
this book is accurate. However, due to differing conditions, tools,
and individual skills, the publisher cannot be responsible for any
injuries, losses, and other damages that may result from the use
of the information in this book.

If you have questions or comments about this book, please contact:
Lark Books
67 Broadway
Asheville, NC 28801
(828) 253-0467

Manufactured in China

ISBN 13: 978-1-60059-037-5
ISBN 10: 1-60059-037-3

For information about custom editions, special sales, premium and corporate
purchases, please contact Sterling Special Sales Department at 800-805-5489 or
specialsales@sterlingpub.com.

Contents

Pearls. They're heavenly—it's hardly surprising we call the entrance to paradise the Pearly Gates! Pearls evoke purity, sophistication, and elegance. Whether decorating the surface of an ancient emperor's imperial robes, embellishing a medieval queen's headpiece, or gracing the neck of a runway starlet, they have withstood fashion's test of time.

Many legendary women have had love affairs with pearls. Grace Kelly, Audrey Hepburn, and Jackie Kennedy wore them as signature ornaments. Cleopatra allegedly dissolved one in vinegar and drank it to show off for Mark Antony. Queen Elizabeth I of England was famously fond of pearls and wore them as badges of her virginity; in portraits, so many of them adorn her gowns, you wonder how she could support the weight. Coco Chanel, perhaps the most influential fashion designer of the twentieth century, declared, "A woman needs ropes and ropes of pearls."

But pearls aren't just the domain of refined high society. They can have fun, too. Josephine Baker, for example, created a sensation in 1926 when she performed at the Folies Bergère in Paris wearing nothing but a girdle of bananas at the waist and strands of pearls around her neck.

As the 30 projects in this book show, pearl jewelry has the ability to go funky and informal, take on understated and traditional tones, or be thoroughly modern. Compare the classic appearance of the Twist ear bobs (page 56) to the contemporary lines of the Golden Crescent earrings (page 96). Both projects, while lovely, have completely different aesthetics.

To make the earrings, bracelets, necklaces, and rings contained in these pages, 19 designers used every shape of pearl: coin, rice, potato, baroque, stick, and more. Depending on their tastes, some chose pearls in natural shades such as white, gray, or black, while others opted for pearls dyed in subtle or eye-popping colors. Pearls pair as well with classic gold (see Nadine Fidelman's pendant on page 92, for example) as they do with shimmery crystals (page 104), vintage silver filigree buttons (page 68), and even the leather cord Diana Light used for her Lasso (page 48). While the focal points of the jewelry are definitely the pearls, the designers also incorporated other materials, from old cameo pins salvaged from the bottoms of jewelry boxes to copper washers found on a hardware store shelf.

The book's first few pages introduce you to pearls and explain how they get created. (Did you know that an oyster can produce only one or two pearls at a time, while the mollusks used in cultivating freshwater pearls yield up to 50 pearls at once?) The next section describes the materials and tools you'll need to get started making jewelry. After that, you'll find basic techniques, such as wireworking, light metalsmithing, and off-loom beading; all are explained in detail, with illustrations to help you succeed at your project. It's a good idea to read that chapter from beginning to end, and then refer back to it whenever needed. Finally come the projects, in which you'll explore techniques as varied as ink stamping (page 73), wire crochet (page 107), and simple stringing, which any beading novice can accomplish with flair. In fact, while a few of the projects might present a slight challenge to anyone who's never beaded at all, almost all of them are downright simple to make...and every one is certainly a little slice of heaven.

Pearl Primer

Left to right: freshwater stick, flat square, and coin pearls

You'll find a vast array of lustrous pearls in *Beading with Pearls.* They come in a wide variety of shapes, colors, and sizes, and when incorporated into the 30 great designs featured, show an amazing range of versatility. You might be surprised to find that their power as a design element is strong, ranging anywhere from lending a soft and delicate whispery tone to giving a bold and colorful shout.

All natural pearls are produced by mollusks. A *naturally-occurring pearl* is created when a piece of sand or other irritant gets inside the mollusk's body and the creature slowly builds layers of smooth *nacre,* a natural secretion also called "mother-of-pearl," around the irritant to make itself more comfortable.

Clockwise from top left: freshwater potato, half-round potato, coin, hybrid teardrop, round, and flat square pearls

Cultured pearls remove the chance factor in finding consistently-sized pearls. They are created by a pearl farmer who inserts a round shell bead inside a mollusk. As in nature, the mollusk builds nacre around the irritant, creating a fairly uniform pearl. Culturing pearls not only garners consistent round sizes, but offers the opportunity to produce other shapes as well. To do so, a pearl farmer plants a shaped shell within a mollusk, and the result is a pearl in that specific shape. Popular pearl shapes include coins, sticks, flat teardrops, squares, and diamonds.

Left to right: freshwater heart, stick, and Baroque pearls

Other types of pearl shapes include *keishi,* which have no nucleus—they are simply the extra nacre that may be produced by a mollusk. *Mabe pearls,* also known as *blister pearls,* are produced by inserting a half bead into a specific place in the mollusk's shell. The mollusk produces a hollow pearl that is removed, filled with glue, and then backed with mother-of-pearl to create a pearl cabochon.

Each species of mollusk creates a slightly different type and color of pearl nacre, but the most noticeable difference is between *freshwater* and *ocean pearls.* Freshwater mollusks produce pearls that have a characteristic uneven surface. They are relatively inexpensive and easy to find at bead shops. Ocean mollusks make pearls that have a very smooth, even surface, but they're harder to come by and are often much more expensive.

Historically, the highest-quality natural pearls have come from southern India and the countries surrounding the Persian Gulf. Japan reigned in overall production for scores of years, but over the last several, China has become the largest producer, offering larger quantities and lower prices.

Top to bottom: glass teardrop; freshwater round, top-drilled oval, rice, two strands of half-round Baroque, rounds, rice, Baroque, button pearls

Other beads made to look like pearls have always been a fashion option, especially for costume jewelry. *Fine glass pearls*, also referred to as *Majorca pearls* in reference to the Mediterranean island where they were first produced in mass quantities, are made of a glass base covered with crushed shells or fish scales. *Crystal pearls* are relative newcomers to beaders' stashes—they consist of a smooth, fine crystal core covered with a pearly coating. *Plastic pearls* are beads covered with opalescent paint and are the least-desirable option for beaders as a seam is often evident, and the finish can chip off during wear.

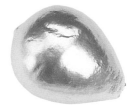

Teardrop pearl

Pearl Purchasing Tips

If your design primarily features pearls or size and shape consistency is crucial, buy the best quality you can find. If your design means that the pearls will be mixed in with dozens of other beads and consistency isn't an issue, you can get away with a less expensive option.

Natural pearls have very small holes, so if your design requires thicker stringing material than the pearl can handle, consider using a pearl reamer to make the holes larger, or buy the larger-holed glass or crystal pearls.

Pearls come in fully-drilled, half-drilled, and un-drilled versions. Make sure to check that you're purchasing the proper type for the project you're making.

Find out how the pearl was colored before you buy it, especially if you plan on using it for a piece of jewelry like a bracelet, which will suffer lots of wear and tear. Most pearls are naturally colored, but some pearls are surface-dyed and the dye will rub off if they're worn frequently.

Getting Started

Before you embark on creating a fabulous piece of pearl jewelry, read on to learn about all the items you need to put it together. Invest in the best materials and tools you can afford to achieve professional results.

Materials

You'll be able to find just about any item included in this materials list at your local high-quality bead shop, but you can also track down these materials online and at most retail bead shows.

Other Beads

Walking into a bead shop for the first time is overwhelming just because of the sheer number of colors, shapes, sizes, and types of beads available. If you fall in love with beads, you'll always be overcome by the "wow" factor, but you don't necessarily need to know about each and every type right away. The Pearl Primer, page 10, covers pearls. The following is a bit of information on the several types of beads, besides pearls, used for the projects in this book.

Crystal beads are made from leaded glass and are cut in a way that produces maximum brilliance. The finest of these beads come from Austria. If you use thread to stitch crystals, buffer the crystals by stringing a seed bead on either side. This helps ensure that the crystal's crisp edges won't cut the thread.

Metal beads can be machine-stamped, made with molds, or handmade. They come in precious and base-metal varieties, including sterling silver, gold-filled, silver- and gold-plated (over brass), vermeil (gold over sterling silver), brass, and pewter.

Seed beads are small glass beads made by cutting long, thin tubes of glass into tiny pieces. The most common sizes are between 6° and 14°(largest to smallest) and they come in a vast array of colors. They are primarily made in the Czech Republic and Japan and come in three popular types: Czech seed beads have a somewhat flat profile, like a donut; Japanese seed beads have a taller profile than Czech seed beads and are fairly uniform from bead to bead; and cylinder beads have thinner walls than other seed beads and are very uniform in shape.

Stringing Materials

The material on which you string beads is crucial to the long, good-looking life of a piece of jewelry. Make sure to use the proper type to keep your creation looking great for years to come.

Beading line, also known as *braided thread,* was developed by the fishing industry. It's a braided nylon thread that's extremely strong and durable, can be knotted, and is a great choice for working with crystal beads because it doesn't abrade easily. It's generally available in clear, white, moss, and dark gray and comes in 6- to 20-pound test weights. Cut this type of thread with child-sized household scissors. Cutting it with embroidery scissors will not only dull the blades but will also make a bad cut.

Beading thread is a very pliable thread made of nylon. It's fairly strong and comes in dozens of colors. Some beading threads come pre-waxed, but if yours doesn't, coat it liberally with wax or thread conditioner (page 19).

Semiprecious stone beads come in every size and shape imaginable; think of any particular kind of semiprecious stone, and there's bound to be a bead made out of it. The types used in this book (rounds and buttons) are fairly easy to find. Most every stone bead is hewn by hand, and the prices range from pennies apiece on up, depending on the availability, grade, and cut of the stone.

Beading thread

Flexible beading wire is primarily used for stringing beads. It's produced by twisting dozens of strands of tiny stainless steel wires together that then receive a nylon coating. Secure this type of wire with crimp beads (page 18).

Leather cord comes in many colors and widths. Much of the cord on the market today isn't really even leather but a type of synthetic. Use scissors to cut the end of leather cord at an angle, and you'll have an easier time stringing beads onto it.

Metal wire is used in this book for wireworking projects ranging from jump rings to ear wires to ring bands. It comes in a range of widths, but 18- to 26-gauge (the smaller the number, the thicker the wire) are the sizes used here. You can purchase all types of metal wire, but the most common ones used to make fine beaded jewelry are sterling silver and gold-filled.

Leather cord

Flexible beading wire

Metal wire

Chain of various sizes

Findings

Beaders call all the little pieces—usually metal—that help keep your jewelry together and secure "findings."

Buttons are often used in beaded designs as one half of a button/loop clasp (see Simple Pleasures on page 82). They can also be a great-looking embellishment.

Chain is made up of connected loops of wire. The loops can come in several forms, including round, oval, twisted, and hammered.

Clasps connect wire ends to keep a necklace or bracelet in place. Here are some of the most common types.

- *Box clasps* have one half that's comprised of a hollow box. The other half is a tab that clicks into the box to lock the clasp.

Left to right: box, toggle, and hook-and-eye clasps

- *Fish hook clasps* are related to hook-and-eye clasps (below). They are shaped like a *J* and are usually used in a design that has a chain at the other end. The clasp hooks into a link of the chain to secure the piece.

- *Hook-and-eye clasps* have one half that's shaped like a hook, the other half like a loop, or "eye." The hook passes through the eye to secure the clasp.

- *Spring ring clasps* are made up of a circle with a small spring-loaded lever that opens and shuts the circle. They are usually small and should be reserved for lightweight pieces.

- *Toggle clasps* have one half that looks like a ring with a loop attached to it; the other half is shaped like a bar with a loop attached to it. Pass the bar through the ring; once the bar lies parallel on top of the ring, you've secured the clasp.

Cones are most often used at the end of a piece of multi-strand jewelry in order to hide knots. They are usually made out of metal and come in a huge variety of designs.

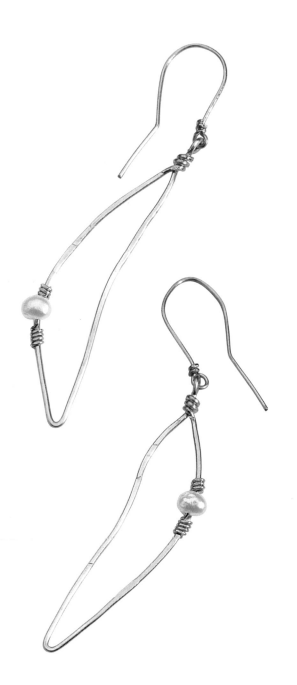

Crimp tubes and crimp beads are used to connect beading wire to a finding. (See page 28 to learn how to use these findings.) Crimp covers are also used in this book—they are beads that open and then close over crimp beads to hide them.

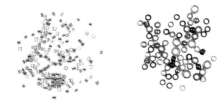

Earring findings are the metal pieces you use to attach an earring design to your earlobe. They include a jump ring-like loop onto which you can add an earring dangle. They come in different shapes, including *French ear wires,* which look like upside-down *U* shapes; and *lever backs,* which are much like French ear wires but have a safety catch on the back to hold the earring in place.

Left, French ear wires; right, lever backs

Eye pins are used in this book to make beaded links. They are made with straight pieces of wire with a simple loop at one end.

Head pins are used for stringing beads to make dangles. Simple head pins are straight wires with a tiny disk at one end to hold beads in place. Ball-end head pins have a sphere at one end.

Left to right, ball-end head pins, regular head pins, eye pins

Jump rings are circular loops of wire used to connect beadwork to findings or findings to findings. They come in open and soldered-closed versions.

Split rings are a more secure form of jump ring. They are formed like tiny key rings.

Other Materials

There are a few other materials you'll need to complete some of the projects in *Beading with Pearls*.

Beeswax and *thread conditioner* are used to prepare thread before stitching. They can help with thread tension and ensure the thread doesn't fray.

Glue is sometimes used to attach metal to metal and other times simply to secure knots. *Jeweler's clear adhesive cement* and *two-part epoxy* are the most popular kinds among beaders.

Patinas used in this book include *liver of sulfur* and *silver black*. They are used to blacken metal, giving it an antiqued look. Make sure to carefully follow the manufacturer's instructions for these products, as many of them are poisonous.

Got Storage?

Once you bring home your beading supplies, there's an inevitable question: Where should you put them? The most important thing is to be able to find them when you need them. So, if you're a person who thrives on organization, take advantage of the loads of bead storage boxes and tubes on the market into which you can park your stash. Organize little storage boxes inside larger ones, keeping similar beads together, all arranged by color.

If you work better with a system of "organized chaos" and are okay with bags, tubes, and boxes of beads scattered willy-nilly, just make certain you know where everything is when you need to call on it. A good tip is to keep together all the materials for a project you're working on, either in a small box or bag. If you wish, keep all the tools you need in there, too—then you can bead wherever you happen to be!

Left to right, thread conditioner, beeswax, adhesive cement

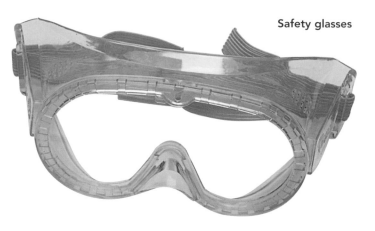

Safety glasses

Tools

Making pearl jewelry requires surprisingly few tools, and all are pretty low-tech. As with other jewelry-making materials, make sure to buy the best type you can afford.

Basic Tools

Chain-nose pliers feature jaws that are flat on the inside but taper to a point on the outside. This type of pliers also comes in a bent version used for grasping hard-to-reach places.

Flat-nose pliers feature jaws that are flat on the inside and have a square nose.

Round-nose pliers feature cylindrical jaws that taper to a very fine point.

Left to right, round-nose, flat-nose, chain-nose, and crimping pliers; wire cutters

Embroidery scissors

Metal hand files

Knitting needles

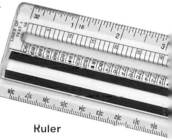

Crimping pliers attach crimp beads and crimp tubes to beading wire. See page 28 for instructions on how to use these pliers.

Jeweler's wire cutters have very sharp blades that come to a point. One side of the pliers leaves a V-shaped cut; the other side leaves a flat, or "flush," cut.

Safety glasses are important to wear when making metal jewelry. They protect your eyes from flying wire pieces.

Dowels and *knitting needles* are called for in this book to make wire coils and form wire into ring bases and ear wires.

Emery boards are used in jewelry making for sanding wire smooth.

Metal hand files, or *needle files,* have very fine teeth. They are used in this book for smoothing wire ends.

Tape measures and *rulers* are used in this book to determine where to cut wire and thread. They are also helpful for checking jewelry lengths and bead and finding sizes. Choose one that has both standard and metric markings.

Ruler

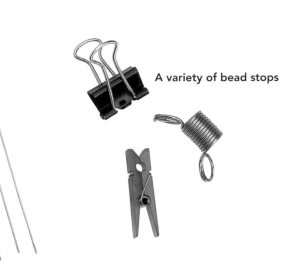

English beading needles

A variety of bead stops

Beading Tools

Bead stops or *strong clips* are used to keep your beads from sliding off the end of your stringing material while you bead. They are most often used with flexible beading wire.

Beading needles are extremely thin pieces of stiff wire (about the width of a piece of thread) that have a tiny hole on one end and a very sharp point on the other. The most popular for beading include *English beading needles*, which are especially thin and long, and *sharp needles*, which have a stronger body and are somewhat shorter.

Embroidery scissors are very sharp scissors with pointed blades. They are used for cutting beading thread.

Thread burners, or *lighters,* help hide the clipped ends of synthetic threads by melting them into a tiny ball. Thread burners are very precise—they have a wire end that, once warmed up, can be placed against the end of the thread and the thread melts away. A lighter does the same job, but it isn't as precise.

Beading mats are used to make sure your beads don't roll off your work surface and onto the floor. Most beaders prefer mats that are made out of the thick, synthetic no-loop fabric used to make the type of blankets often found in hotels. Dishcloths or pieces of felt work well, too.

Thread burner

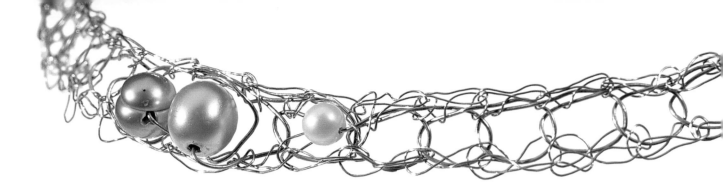

Special Tools

Jeweler's hammers are used in this book for flattening, hardening, and texturizing wire.

Steel blocks, or *bench blocks*, are thick, smooth chunks of steel upon which you can hammer wire.

Vises are very heavy clamps that are often mounted to a work bench. Use this tool for holding pieces in place while you drill or hammer them.

Ring mandrels are long, slightly tapered cylinders of hard metal. They have ring sizes marked down the side so you can make a ring band to fit.

Bead reamers are pointed diamond-tipped tools that, when rotated within a bead, can widen the hole. They come in very handy for pearls, which have especially small holes.

Drills and *drill bits* are used to make holes in beads and flat pieces of metal. A small craft drill is best suited for jewelry making.

Polishing cloths are pieces of soft material that have been infused with a chemical to shine metal. They can be found at most bead shops or fine jewelry stores.

Crochet hooks are most often made of metal and have a pointed hook at one end to work the thread (or wire) in crochet.

Crochet hook

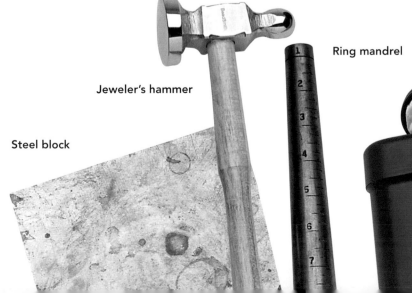

Ring mandrel

Jeweler's hammer

Steel block

Polishing cloth

Basic Techniques

It really *is* easy to make your own beautiful pearl jewelry, even if you're new to beading. There are dozens of beading techniques, but only a handful you'll need to know to complete the projects in *Beading with Pearls.* Just refer to the following step-by-step techniques, and you'll be up and running in no time. If you're an experienced jewelry maker, you'll likely find this section important, too. As you know, there's always something new to learn in beading, and it's good to have a refresher for those techniques that have gone a little fuzzy in your bag of beading tricks.

Wireworking

You'll only need to know the following techniques to bend and shape wire into the beautiful wirework creations featured in this book.

Flush cutting wire involves using the flat, or flush, side of the wire cutters to make the cut so the wire end is flat.

Filing and *sanding* are necessary for smoothing rough wire ends. Use a flat metal file or emery paper to achieve this, touching the wire occasionally as you go to check for any rough spots.

Coiling, or tightly wrapping, wire is primarily used in this book for attaching one wire to another, creating decorative coils, and making jump rings. Start by grasping the base (a thick wire, dowel, or knitting needle) tightly in one hand. Hold the wrapping wire with your other hand and make one wrap. Reposition your hands so you can continue to wrap the wire around the base wire, making right revolutions (photo 1).

Setting Up Your Workspace

Just like arranging your space for cooking, writing a letter, potting a plant, or even settling down for a good book, you need to set up your space for beading. The main thing to consider is what type of beading you'll be doing: Will you need a hard surface onto which you can hammer or drill? Do you need to sit upright at a table where you can spread out an array of hand tools and do wirework? Or do you just need a comfy chair and a beading mat to work off-loom beading? Whatever type of space you require, the top priority is good lighting—you don't want to compromise your number one tool, your eyes.

photo 1

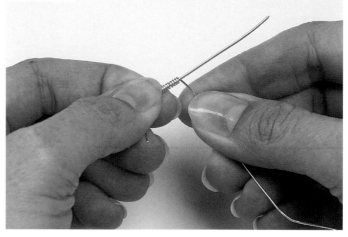

photo 2

Wire spirals are used primarily for decoration, but can also be used to keep beads from sliding off the end of wire. Begin by using round-nose pliers to make a small loop at the end of the wire. Use chain- or flat-nose pliers to grasp the loop flat within the jaws so the edge of the loop sticks out slightly. Use your fingers to push the straight wire so it curves around the loop (photo 2). Adjust the wire's position within the pliers so you can curve more wire around the spiral. Repeat until you reach the desired width (photo 3).

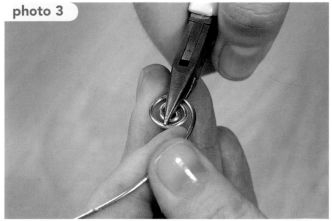

photo 3

Opening and Closing Rings

Always open a jump ring with two pairs of pliers, one positioned on each side of the split. Push one pair of pliers away from you, and pull the other one toward you (photo 4). This way the ring will be opened laterally, instead of horizontally, which can weaken the wire. (You'll also open any other wire loop this way.)

photo 4

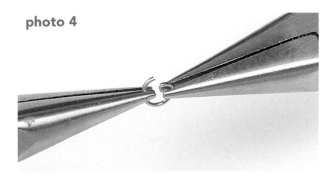

Making Your Own Jump Rings

When you create your own jump rings, you'll find you have yet another flexible design option at your fingertips. Using the exact size and material you desire gives a world of possibilities.

1. Tightly and evenly coil a length of wire around the dowel. The more coils you make, the more jump rings you'll end up with.

2. Slide the wire off the dowel. Stretch the coil slightly to create space between each rotation (figure 1).

3. Use the flush side of the cutters to cut one coil off of the spring. Pick up the ring and face the cutters the other way to snip the other wire tip flush (figure 2).

Wire loops come in two versions, *simple* and *wrapped.*

Start a *simple loop* by using chain-nose pliers to make a 90° bend ⅜ inch (9 mm) from the end of the wire; or, if you're using the loop to secure a bead (as with a bead dangle), make a 90° bend right at the top of the bead and cut the wire to ⅜ inch (9 mm), as in photo 5.

Use round-nose pliers to grasp the wire end and roll the pliers until the wire touches the 90° bend (photo 6).

fig. 1

fig. 2

photo 5

photo 6

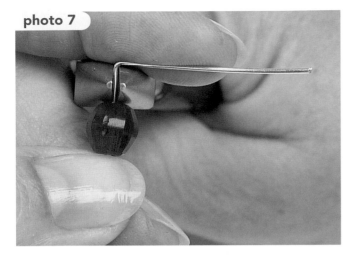

photo 7

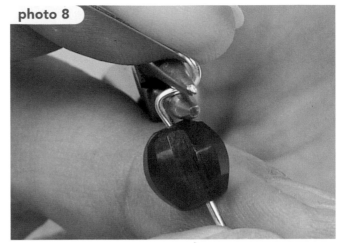

photo 8

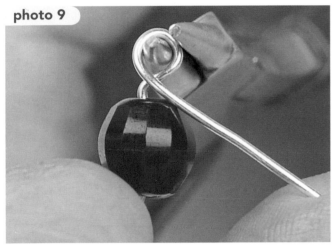

photo 9

photo 10

Begin a *wrapped loop* by using chain-nose pliers to make a 90° bend in the wire 2 inches (3.9 mm) from one wire end (or ¼ inch [6 mm] from the top of a bead) (photo 7).

Use round-nose pliers to grasp the bend and shape the wire over the pliers' top jaw (photo 8).

Reposition the pliers so the bottom jaw is in the loop and swing the wire underneath to form a loop (photo 9).

Use chain-nose pliers or your fingers to wrap the wire in a tight coil down the stem (photo 10). Trim the excess wire close to the wrap, and use chain-nose pliers to tighten the wire end.

You can easily and securely attach a wrapped loop to another loop or chain link. First form the loop, pass the wire end through the place you want to attach it, and then make the wrap. The loops will be permanently attached. (See Honey Drizzle, page 39, for an illustration of this technique.)

Stringing

Stringing beads is a simple act—simply pass the thread or wire through a bead, and you've got it! It's how you arrange beads on the stringing material that creates masterpieces—that's what takes practice.

Crimping wire is a stringing technique used to attach wire to a finding (like a clasp). Start by stringing one crimp bead and the finding. Pass the wire back through the crimp bead in the opposite direction. Next, slide the crimp bead against the finding so it's snug, but not so tight that the wire can't move freely. Squeeze the crimp bead with the back U-shaped notch in a pair of crimping pliers (photo 11).

Turn the crimp bead at a 90° angle, and nestle it into the front notch. Gently squeeze the bead so it collapses on itself into a nicely-shaped tube (photo 12).

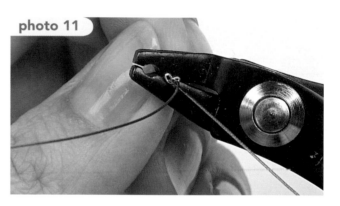

photo 11

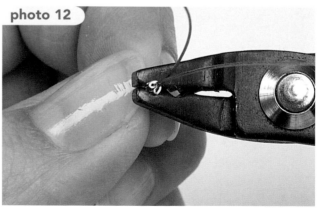

photo 12

Knotting

Knowing how to tie knots is very important if you're working off-loom beading, but the skill will come in handy for other beading as well.

Overhand knots are formed by making a loop with the thread, passing the thread end through the loop, and pulling tight (figure 1).

fig. 1

Slipknots are used in this book for starting beaded wire crochet. Form a loose overhand knot (above), but before you tighten it, use a crochet hook to catch a small loop of the stringing material (figure 2) and pull it through the center of the knot (figure 3).

fig. 2   **fig. 3**

Square knots are formed by first making an overhand knot, right end over left end, and finishing with another overhand knot, this time left end over right end (figure 4).

fig. 4

Surgeon's knots are extremely secure square knots. They are basically made the same way as a square knot, but when you make your first overhand knot, wrap the thread around itself a few times before passing it through the loop. Finish the knot with another overhand knot and pull tight (figure 5).

fig. 5

Off-Loom Beading

Off-loom beading refers to a large family of beading techniques that don't require a loom to create a smooth "fabric" of seed beads—just a needle and thread. There are dozens of ways to stitch beads together, but you'll only need to know a few by heart to complete the projects in this book.

fig. 6

Simple fringe is a type of beaded embellishment made by stringing on a length of beads and, skipping the last bead strung, passing the needle back through the rest of the beads just strung (figure 6).

Ladder stitch is often used to make a foundation row for brick or herringbone stitch. Begin by stringing two beads. Pass through the beads again to make a circle and manipulate them so they sit side by side (figure 7).

String one bead and pass down through the second bead initially strung and up through the one just strung. Repeat to add one bead at a time until you reach the desired length (figure 8).

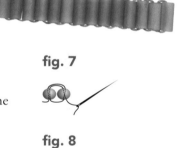

fig. 7

fig. 8

General Off-Loom Beading Terms and Techniques

Pass through means you'll pass the needle through the beads in the same direction as they were strung. *Pass back through* means you'll go through in the opposite direction.

You've made a *row* of off-loom beadwork when you've stitched beads in a line back and forth, and it results in a flat piece of beadwork. A *round* is created when you've stitched beads in circles, creating circular or tubular pieces of beadwork.

A *stop*, or *tension*, bead is used at the end of a working thread to keep beads from slipping off the end of the thread. To make one, simply string a bead and pass through it again once or twice. Once you've worked your piece enough that the beads are secure, you can easily remove the stop bead.

The *tail thread* is the length at the end of the thread that remains below the first bead you strung. The *working thread* is the portion of thread between the needle and the first beads strung. You use it to do your stitching.

To *end a thread*, weave through several beads on the body of the beadwork, tie an overhand knot on the threads between beads, pass through a few more beads to hide the knot, and trim the knot close to the work. You also use this technique to secure the thread when you're finishing a piece.

To *start a new thread*, thread a needle with the required length of thread. Pass through several beads on the body of the beadwork, tie an overhand knot between beads as desired, and continue to weave through the beads until you exit from a place where you can keep stitching.

Weaving through beads on an off-loom piece of beadwork means you're passing the needle through beads on the body of the beadwork so you can exit elsewhere. Keep your thread hidden by passing only through adjacent beads.

To *reinforce* off-loom beadwork, simply pass through the stitched beads more times than is required. This stiffens and strengthens the work.

Square stitch produces a relatively stiff beaded fabric in which all the beads sit side by side to create a grid. Start by stringing a base row of beads long enough to make up your first row. Begin the second row by stringing one bead and passing through the last bead strung on the previous row and the bead just strung.

The two beads just worked should sit side by side. String one bead and pass through the next bead on the base row and the bead just strung (figure 9). Continue across the base strand, stitching one bead to one bead until you reach the end.

fig. 9

fig. 10

Start the next row by stringing one bead and stitching it to the last bead added on the previous row (as you did with the first row). Working in the opposite direction from the first row, continue across, stitching one bead to one bead (figure 10).

Easy Beginner
PROJECTS

Victoria

Garner lots of compliments from a multi-strand bracelet that's quick to make. Its Victorian-era style makes it look like a family heirloom, but the stretchy elastic used to string the pearls makes it anything but starchy— it's very comfortable to wear.

Designer: Diana Light

Finished Size

6¾ inches (17.1 cm)

Materials

Approximately 115 yellow freshwater pearls, 6-mm half-round potato

1 golden marble cameo brooch with brass filigree, 27 x 38 mm

36-inch (91.4 cm) length of .5-mm clear stretch cord

Tools

Scissors

Ruler

Techniques

Knotting (page 29)

Instructions

1. Cut four 9-inch (22.9 cm) lengths of cord.

2. String enough pearls on the cord to measure 6¾ inches (17.1 cm). Tie the cord ends into three tight square knots, making a stretchy circle of beads (figure 1). Trim the cord ends close to the beads.

3. Repeat step 2 three more times to make four stretchy bracelets.

4. Gather all of the stretchy bracelets together so the knots are all in the same place. Open the pin back on the brooch and pass the pin over each of the four knots (figure 2). Close the pin back.

fig. 1

fig. 2

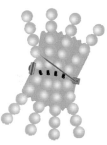

Three-Ring Circ-ul-us

This pearl ring is a great example of contemporary jewelry design. Despite its simple construction, it looks quite sophisticated.

Designer: Cynthia B. Wuller

Materials

1 white freshwater pearl, 8½- to 9-mm half-drilled, half-round

7¾ inches (19.7 cm) length of 20-gauge, dead-soft, gold-filled wire

Jeweler's cement

Tools

Metal ring mandrel

Vise

Ruler

Safety glasses

Chain-nose pliers

Wire cutters

Chasing hammer

Techniques

Coiling wire (page 24)

Instructions

1. Secure the ring mandrel in the vise.

2. Measure ½ inch (1.3 cm) in from one end of the wire. Use chain-nose pliers to make a 90° bend at that measurement, making a short wire tail.

3. Put on the safety glasses. Place the tail perpendicularly on the mandrel. Move the wire to a position on the mandrel that's a half size smaller than your desired size. Use one hand to keep the tail at that measurement while you wrap the loose wire end around the mandrel three times (figure 1).

4. Keeping the wire on the mandrel, use chain-nose pliers to grasp all three wraps. Pull the loose end of the wire toward the tail and make a 90° bend, this one parallel to the mandrel (figure 2).

5. Tightly coil the loose end of the wire around the tail twice (figure 3). Trim the loose wire close to the wrap, and use chain-nose pliers to tighten.

6. Take the ring off the mandrel and slightly spread the ring band's wires apart, creating a ⅛-inch (3 mm) gap between each band.

fig. 1

fig. 2

fig. 3

7. Place the ring back on the mandrel and hammer the three bands to create texture and to enlarge the ring to the correct size. When you are halfway through hammering, take the ring off the mandrel, flip it so the back band is now in front, and put it back on the mandrel; this will keep the band symmetrical. Adjust the bands with chain-nose pliers if they become crooked while hammering.

8. Remove the ring from the mandrel. Trim the tail wire to ⅛ inch (3 mm). Place the pearl on the tail to check that it's the correct height—the bottom of the pearl should be flush with the coiled section. Cut down the wire, if necessary. Remove the pearl and fill the hole with glue. Put the pearl back onto the wire and hold it in place for one minute. Let it dry on the mandrel for 10 to 15 minutes. Remove the ring from the mandrel and let the glue cure overnight.

Honey Drizzle

This three-strand necklace is a great project to highlight a collection of orphan beads and chains from your stash. The clasp is embellished, which gives you the option to wear the toggle up front.

Designer: Janet A. Lasher

Finished Size

20 inches (50.8 cm)

Materials

5 white freshwater pearls,
10-mm potato

16 golden freshwater pearls,
8-mm half-round potato

8 semiprecious citrine nuggets, 12 mm

16 semiprecious faceted African opal
rounds, 5 mm

15 topaz and light topaz crystals in
assorted shapes, 3 to 12 mm

6 gold-filled or sterling silver jump
rings, 5 mm

1 gold-filled or sterling silver head pin,
3 inches (7.6 cm) long

1 gold-filled or sterling silver toggle
clasp, 25 mm

Assorted gold-filled or sterling silver
chain remnants, 45 inches (1.1 m) total

5-foot (1.5 m) length of 24-gauge,
gold-filled or sterling silver wire

Silver black or other patina

Paper towel

Instructions

1. Cut the 24-gauge wire into pieces, each approximately 12 inches (30.8 cm) long. Set aside.

2. Prepare the patina according to the manufacturer's instructions. Dip the jump rings, head pin, clasp, chain, and wire into the patina. Once you reach the desired effect, remove the pieces and rinse with clear water. Let air dry on a paper towel. *Note:* Don't immerse the beads into the patina; it may permanently remove the nacre on the pearls and mar the surfaces of stones and other beads. Polish each piece of wire, chain, clasp, and head pin with a polishing pad or extra-fine steel wool to achieve an antique look.

3. Run each wire piece through the wire-straightening pliers. This straightens and tempers the wire at the same time. Cut the wire into 3- to 4-inch (7.6 to 10.2 cm) pieces and set aside.

4. Slide a 5-mm crystal and an 8-mm pearl on the head pin. Form a simple loop to secure the beads. Pick up one of the wire pieces and make a wrapped loop at one end that attaches to the simple loop you just created. String on one citrine nugget and form a wrapped loop to secure it (figure 1). Set the dangle aside.

fig. 1

5. Cut the chain remnants into pieces, each 1 to 2 inches (2.5 to 5.1 cm) long.

6. Utilize the bead design board to make a random arrangement of chains and beads or sets of beads, being sure to begin and end the sequence with a chain. Keep in mind that this is a three-strand necklace—each strand can be the same length or you can create a layered look by linking the upper and lower strands off of the middle length of chain. Design all three strands at the same time to achieve a good distribution of chains and beads across the length of the necklace.

fig. 2

7. Use a jump ring to attach one half of the clasp to the end link of the first chain. Form a wrapped loop on the end of one of the wire pieces that attaches to the end link at the other end of this chain. String on the first bead or set of beads in your arrangement and form a wrapped loop that attaches to the end link of the next chain (figure 2). Repeat across to complete the middle strand. Use one jump ring to attach the other half of the clasp to the end link of the last chain.

fig. 3

8. Repeat step 7 to create the second and third strands (figure 3).

9. Attach the dangle to the jump ring at the ring end of the necklace.

10. Check all the wrapped loops for clean cuts and tucked-in wire ends. If desired, use the polishing pad to polish the chains and toggle.

Swingset

Sassy and bold, these earrings incorporate a little elementary metalsmithing with simple wirework. Any type of pearl will do, but the coin shape lends a definite swingin' '60s attitude.

Designer: Andrea McLester

Finished Size

2½ inches (6.4 cm) long

Materials

2 rose freshwater pearls, 13 mm coin

2 sterling silver 22-gauge, ball-end head pins, 1½ inches (3.1 cm) long

1 mm x 3 mm rectangular sterling silver wire, 3½ inches (8.9 cm)

3-inch (7.6 cm) length of 20-gauge, round, sterling silver wire

Tools

Wire cutters

Ball peen hammer

Bench block or other smooth, hard, metal surface

Metal file, emery board, or sandpaper

Fine-point permanent marker

Small finishing nail

Safety glasses

Drill with a 1-mm bit

Drill press (optional)

Chain-nose pliers

Round-nose pliers

½-inch (1.3 cm) wooden dowel, 4 inches (10.2 cm) long

Silver cream or polishing cloth

Techniques

Simple loop (page 26)

Wrapped loop (page 27)

Opening and closing loops (page 25)

Instructions

1. Cut the rectangular wire into two 1¾-inch (4.5 cm) pieces. Set aside.

2. Cut the 20-gauge wire into two 1½-inch (3.1 cm) pieces. Set aside.

3. Place one of the rectangular wire pieces on the block. Use the ball end of the hammer to strike the wire's face repeatedly to create texture. Disperse your hammer blows equally along both sides. You may notice the wire curving sideways because one side of the metal has been hammered more than the other. To correct this, simply hammer along the inside of the curve and the metal will gradually straighten.

4. Use the metal file, emery board, or sandpaper to file the ends of the hammered wire. The ends should be smooth and the corners rounded.

5. Mark a small dot on the hammered wire 2 mm from each end. Use the hammer and small finishing nail to make a dimple, or pilot hole, on each dot (figure 1). The blow should be hard enough to dent the metal but not so hard as to puncture it.

fig. 1

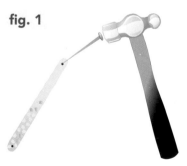

6. If you have a drill press available, set the drill into it (the press makes for precision drilling). Put on the safety glasses. Turn on the drill and lower the end of the bit directly into the pilot hole, keeping the drill perpendicular to the silver wire.

7. File any metal burrs off the back of the wires. Set the hammered wire aside.

8. Form a simple loop at the end of one of the 20-gauge wire pieces. Use your thumb to hold the loop against the wooden dowel as you wrap the rest of the wire halfway around the dowel (figure 2). Use chain-nose pliers to make a slight bend in the wire about ³⁄₁₆ inch (5 mm) from the end. Make the bend so it angles away from the inside curve. File the end of the wire smooth.

fig. 2

9. Attach the ear wire to the hammered wire. Set aside.

10. Slip a pearl onto a head pin. Form a wrapped loop that attaches to the open hole of the hammered wire.

11. Repeat steps 3 through 10 to make a second earring. Polish the earrings with silver cream or a polishing cloth.

This ensemble design features swirling silver wire peppered with beautiful blue coin pearls.

Arabesque

Designer: Pat Evans

Finished Size

Necklace, 24¼ inches (62 cm);
earrings, 2 inches (5.1 cm)

Materials

15 royal blue freshwater pearls,
13-mm coin

2 sterling silver earring findings

47-inch (1.2 m) length of 18-gauge,
twisted sterling silver wire

42-inch (1.1 m) length of 21-gauge,
dead-soft, round sterling silver wire

Tools

Polishing cloth

Flush cutters

Round-nose pliers

Chain-nose pliers

Flat-nose pliers

Techniques

Simple loop (page 26)

Wire spiral (page 25)

Wrapped loop (page 27)

Opening and closing rings (page 25)

Instructions

1. Pull the 18-gauge wire through a polishing cloth to clean and straighten it. Cut the wire into 14 pieces, each 3 inches (7.6 cm) long. Set aside.

2. Take one of the pieces of 18-gauge wire and use the tip of the round-nose pliers to make a small loop at one end. Make another small loop at the other end of the wire, this time turning the loop so it curves in the opposite direction from the first one (figure 1). Hold one of the small loops in the flat-nose pliers and make one rotation to create a loose spiral. Repeat on the other wire end, this time spiraling in the opposite direction so you make an *S* shape (figure 2). Use your fingers to refine the shape as needed. Repeat this step to make 14 *S*-links in all. Set aside.

   fig. 1   **fig. 2**

3. Cut 1½ inches (3.8 cm) of 18-gauge wire. Grasp one end of the wire in the largest part of the jaws of the round-nose pliers and form a loop. The cut end of the loop should touch the midpoint of the wire. Form another loop on the other end of the wire, this time turning the loop so it curves in the direction opposite the first one, making a figure eight-shaped clasp eye (figure 3). Set aside.

   fig. 3

4. Cut a 3-inch (7.6 cm) piece of 18-gauge wire. Use round-nose pliers to form a small loop on each end of the wire. This time both loops should be on the same side of the wire. Form the top half of an *S*-link at one end of the wire as you did in step 2. Use the largest part of the jaws of the round-nose pliers to bend the center of the wire into a *U* shape. Use round-nose pliers to curve up a small *U* shape at the straight end of the wire to make a hook clasp (figure 4). Set it aside.

   fig. 4

5. Pull the 21-gauge wire through a polishing cloth to clean and straighten it. Cut the wire into 15 pieces, each 2¾ inches (7 cm) long. Set aside.

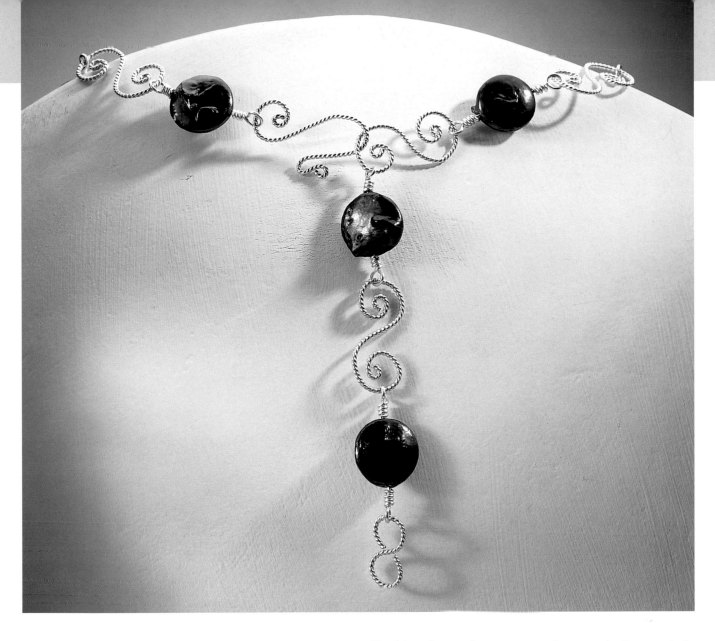

6. String a pearl onto a piece of 21-gauge wire. Form a wrapped loop at one end of the wire that attaches to one loop of the clasp eye. Form a wrapped loop at the other end of the wire that attaches to one end of an *S*-link. Continue connecting beaded links to *S*-links until you have added 13 beaded links and 12 *S*-links. End the chain by connecting the last beaded link to the hook clasp.

7. To make matching earrings, shape a tight 5-mm spiral at one end of one of the remaining pieces of 21-gauge wire. String on a coin pearl. Form a wrapped loop at the straight end of the wire that attaches to one of the *S*-links. Attach the other end of the *S*-link to an ear wire. Repeat to make a second earring, this time connecting the *S*-link to the ear wire so it faces in the opposite direction of the first earring.

Lasso

Versatile to wear, this easy-to-make piece can be worn as a necklace, bracelet, lariat, or belt. Because the knots and pearls "lock" into one another, the piece is surprisingly secure when worn.

Designer: Diana Light

Finished Size

4 feet (1.2 m)

Materials

11 white freshwater pearls,
6.5- to 7-mm round

19 white freshwater pearls,
5-mm round

30 sterling silver 24-gauge head pins,
1½ inches (3.8 cm) long

67-inch (1.7 m) length of 1.5 mm dark
brown, Greek-style leather cord

Tools

Chain-nose pliers

Round-nose pliers

Wire cutters

Ruler

Techniques

Wrapped loop (page 27)

Knotting (page 29)

Instructions

1. Slide a pearl onto a head pin. Make a wrapped loop to secure the pearl, but instead of trimming the wire end, keep wrapping the wire around the top of the pearl to make a small, spiral bead cap (figure 1). *Note:* Be sure to make the loop on each dangle large enough to string onto the leather cord.

   fig. 1

2. Repeat step 1, using all of the pearls and head pins, so you end up with 30 pearl dangles. Set aside.

   fig. 2

3. At the end of the leather cord, tie an overhand knot that incorporates one of the dangles in it (figure 2).

4. String one or two dangles onto the cord. Measure 1¾ inches to 2 inches (4.5 cm to 5.1 cm) down the cord and tie an overhand knot.

5. Repeat step 4 down the length of the cord, sometimes randomly stringing on dangles between knots and other times incorporating the dangles into the knots as in step 3. Be sure to tie all the knots in the same direction.

Circles and Squares

Although the majority of the materials for this bracelet can be found at a hardware store rather than a high-end bead shop, it exudes a Modernist's sophistication. This version features flat square pearls, but coins would work well, too.

Designer: Pat Evans

Finished Size

7¾ inches (19.7 cm)

Materials

5 rose-copper freshwater pearls, 12-mm flat square

5 copper washers, outside diameter 1 inch (2.5 cm), inside diameter ⅝ inch (1.6 cm)

15-inch (38.1 cm) length of 22-gauge, dead soft, round copper wire

33-inch (83.8 cm) length of 16-gauge, dead soft, round copper wire

Tools

0000 steel wool

Tumbler with stainless steel shot and burnishing liquid (optional)

Flush cutters

Bent-tip chain-nose pliers

2 chain-nose pliers

Round-nose pliers

⅜-inch (9 mm) dowel, 4 inches (10.2 cm)

Chasing hammer

Bench block

Techniques

Wrapped loop (page 27)

Making jump rings (page 26)

Opening and closing rings (page 25)

Instructions

1. Clean the washers and remove the sharp edges on the underside by polishing them with steel wool or by tumbling them for 30 to 60 minutes. Dry the washers and set them aside.

2. Straighten and smooth the 22-gauge wire by pulling it through the steel wool. Cut the wire into five 3-inch (7.6 cm) pieces. Set them aside.

3. String one pearl on to a piece of 22-gauge wire. Slide the pearl to the middle of the wire and center a copper washer horizontally underneath the pearl.

4. Use your non-dominant hand to keep the pearl and washer in place as you grasp one wire end and make a sharp bend down the side and underneath the washer. Use bent-tip chain-nose pliers to guide the wire up through the center of the washer (figure 1). Make one tight wrap around the wire as in a wrapped loop (figure 2). Repeat this step for the other wire end. Finish seating the pearl by making a wrap with one wire end; repeat on the other side. This will help you easily center the pearl inside the washer (figure 3). Trim any excess wire and use chain-nose pliers to tighten the wraps. Repeat with the remaining 22-gauge wire, washers, and pearls to make five beaded links in all. Set them aside.

fig. 1

fig. 2

fig. 3

5. Cut a 3-inch (7.6 cm) length of 16-gauge wire and set it aside. Use the rest of the 16-gauge wire to make 19 jump rings in all. If you have extra jump rings, select only the roundest ones for this project.

6. Hammer each jump ring two or three times on its front and back. If the ring opens as you hammer, gently reshape it using the same technique as for opening and closing jump rings. Set the jump rings aside.

7. Straighten and polish the 3-inch (7.6 cm) length of 16-gauge wire cut in step 5. Use round-nose pliers to form a ¼-inch (6 mm) loop at one end. Shape the center of the wire over the dowel in a *U* shape. Form another, slightly smaller, loop on the straight end of the wire (figure 4). Hammer this wire fish-hook clasp to flatten and harden the metal.

fig. 4

8. Position the beaded links on the work surface so the 22-gauge wires line up. Use two jump rings to attach the large loop of the clasp to the left side of the first beaded link, one jump ring on each side of the wrapped loop.

9. Attach two jump rings to the right side of the previous beaded link. Open two more jump rings and use them to connect the two jump rings just added and the left side of the next beaded link in the line up. Repeat until you've attached all the links. Finish by adding one jump ring to the left side of the last link.

Pearl Bouquet

Delicate pearl bouquets make wonderful adornments for any lobe. Create these earrings by linking beaded dangles to a short chain.

Pearl Bouquet

Designer: Lisa M. Call

Finished Size

1 inch (2.5 cm)

Materials

2 white freshwater pearls, 5 x 7-mm top-drilled teardrop

2 white freshwater pearls, 5-mm keishi

2 white freshwater pearls, 5-mm round

2 mauve freshwater pearls, 5-mm button

2 peach freshwater pearls, 5-mm button

2 mauve freshwater pearls, 4-mm round

2 white freshwater pearls, 4-mm button

2 peach freshwater pearls, 3-mm round

2 white topaz or quartz faceted rondelles, 3 mm

14 sterling silver 24-gauge head pins, 1½ inches (3.8 cm) long

2 sterling silver 24-gauge ball-end head pins, 1½ inches (3.8 cm) long

2 sterling silver lever back or French hook earring findings

2-inch (5.1 cm) length of 2.5-mm oval link sterling silver chain

9-inch (22.9 cm) length of 26-gauge sterling silver wire

Instructions

1. Cut the chain into two 1-inch (2.5 cm) pieces. Set aside.

2. Cut two 4½-inch (11.4 cm) pieces of wire. Set aside.

3. String one top-drilled pearl onto a piece of wire. Let the pearl slide one-third of the way down the wire. Cross the wire ends at the top of the pearl to form a triangle.

4. Use chain-nose pliers to grasp the short wire where the two wires cross. Bend the short wire so it points straight up from the top of the pearl. Bend the long wire so it sits at a 90° angle from the short wire (figure 1).

fig. 1

5. Tightly wrap the long wire around the short wire one time. Continue to coil the wire down toward the pearl to make a cone shape (figure 2). Trim the long wire and use chain-nose pliers to tighten the wrap.

fig. 2

6. Make a wrapped loop with the short wire that attaches to the end link of one of the chains. Continue making the wrap until it meets the beginning of the coil you made in the previous step (figure 3). Attach the other end of the chain to an ear wire.

fig. 3

7. Slide a 5-mm white pearl onto a regular head pin. Make a wrapped loop that attaches to the fifth link on the chain (the same link that holds the teardrop pearl dangle). Slip a 5-mm peach pearl onto a regular head pin. Make a wrapped loop that attaches to the same chain link, this time on the other side of the teardrop dangle. Continue adding two pearl dangles to each chain link, adding one 5-mm mauve pearl dangle and one keishi pearl dangle on the fourth link. (*Note:* Use a ball-end head pin to make the keishi dangle so it resembles a flower.) Add one 4-mm white pearl dangle and one 4-mm mauve pearl dangle to the third link; add one 3-mm peach pearl dangle and one white topaz dangle to the second link.

8. Repeat steps 3 through 7 to make a second earring.

Twist

A thin, spiralling wire cages a large pearl, creating the perfect earring dangle. Experiment with wire and pearl types and the number of spiral rotations used— you'll find an array of looks at your fingertips.

Designer: Jean Power

Finished Size

1³⁄₁₆ inch (20 mm)

Materials

2 cream freshwater pearls, ½-inch
(1.3 cm) long oval

2 sterling silver earring findings

12-inch (30.5 cm) length of 22-gauge,
sterling silver wire

Tools

Wire cutters

Ruler or measuring tape

Round-nose pliers

Chain- or flat-nose pliers

Techniques

Wrapped loop (page 27)

Coiling wire (page 24)

Opening and closing rings (page 25)

Instructions

1. Cut the wire into two 6-inch (15.2 cm) pieces.
   Set aside.

2. Take one of the pieces of wire and use round-nose
   pliers to form a ³⁄₁₆-inch (4 mm) *U*-shaped bend at
   one end. Use chain-nose pliers to squish the shape
   together (figure 1).

3. String a pearl onto the bent wire. Make a wrapped
   loop to secure the pearl.

4. Continue wrapping the wire around the top of the
   pearl until you have four to five coils (figure 2).

5. Make two loose spirals around the pearl to reach the
   bottom. Coil the remainder of the wire down the
   bend you made in step 2, leaving the tip of the bend
   exposed (figure 3). If desired, wrap the wire over
   itself to give the coil a heftier look. Trim any excess
   wire and use chain-nose pliers to tighten the wrap.

6. Attach an earring finding to the wrapped loop.

7. Repeat steps 2 through 6 to make a second earring.

fig. 1

fig. 2

fig. 3

Chlorophyll

A bold jewelry statement, this piece
is a great illustration of how versatile
pearls can be. Not all pearl jewelry is
delicate and refined; it can be funky
and chunky, too. This bracelet is simple
to make and wonderful to wear.

Chlorophyll

Designer: Diana Light

Finished Size

6¾ inches (17.1 cm)

Materials

96 freshwater pearls, 10-mm teardrop in three shades of green

2 gold five-hole spacer bars, 1 inch (2. 5 cm)

60-inch (1.5 m) length of .5 mm clear elastic stretch cord

Tools

Scissors

Ruler

Techniques

Knotting (page 29)

Instructions

1. Cut six 10-inch (25.4 cm) lengths of cord.

2. Tie an overhand knot at one end of one of the cords. String eight green pearls of the same shade and pass through the third hole of one of the spacer bars. String eight more of the same-colored pearls and pass through the first hole of another spacer bar. Tie the cord ends into three tight square knots, making a stretchy circle of beads (figure 1). Trim the elastic close to the beads.

3. Repeat step 2 five more times, each time changing the spacer-bar holes to create twists in the bracelet (figure 2). Because there are six strands, you will need to use two of the spacer-bar holes twice.

fig. 1

fig. 2

Cyclone

A few wireworking techniques are all you need to know to whip up this eye-catching ring. Change the pearl type and experiment with different-shaped spirals and you'll have a completely new look.

Designer: Katherine Song

Finished Size

Ring top, 1 inch (2.5 cm)

Materials

3 burgundy freshwater pearls,
6-mm potato

20-inch (50.8 cm) length of 20-gauge,
silver-plated craft wire

10-inch (25.4 cm) length of 26-gauge,
silver-plated craft wire

Tools

Wire cutters

Ruler

Ring mandrel

Round-nose pliers

Flat-nose pliers

Techniques

Coiling wire (page 24)

Wire spiral (page 25)

Instructions

1. Measure 7 inches (17.8 cm) down the 20-gauge wire length. Place the wire on the mandrel at that point. Tightly coil the longer end of wire around the mandrel four times to make a ring base. Pass the wire through the ring base and wrap it around all four wire rotations to secure the base. This is the point where your ring top will sit.

2. Pass the 26-gauge wire through the ring base below the ring's top point. Once you've reached the middle of the 26-gauge wire, make two wraps around the ring base (figure 1).

fig. 1

3. String a pearl onto the 26-gauge wire. Hold the wire about ½ inch (1.3 cm) from the ring base and bend the wire down. Twist the wire onto itself four to five times to make a stem (figure 2). Wrap around the base twice and make another pearl stem. Repeat one more time to make three pearl stems in all.

fig. 2

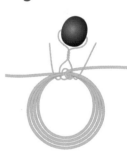

4. Coil the 7-inch (17.8 cm) end of the 20-gauge wire two or three times around one of the pearl stems and once around the ring base. Use the same wire to repeat for the other two stems.

5. Create a spiral on each end of the 20-gauge wire. Arrange the spirals so they are on different sides of the ring top.

6. Repeat step 5 using the 26-gauge wire. Arrange all of the spirals to your liking.

Tuxedo

Perfect for a fancy event, these simple and elegant earrings use plain wire to highlight the beauty of the pearls. Let your pearls swing!

Designer: Jean Power

Finished Size

1¾ inches (4.4 cm)

Materials

2 lavender iris freshwater pearls, 10-mm potato

6-inch (15.2 cm) length of 20-gauge sterling silver wire

2 sterling silver earring findings

Tools

Bead reamer, optional

Ruler or measuring tape

Wire cutters

Bead tube or 1/2-inch (1.3 cm) dowel, 4 inches (10.2 cm) long

Round-nose pliers

Chain- or flat-nose pliers

Techniques

Simple loop (page 26)

Opening and closing rings (page 25)

Instructions

Note: You may need to use a bead reamer to enlarge the holes in your pearls if they don't fit on the 20-gauge wire. If you don't have a bead reamer, make the earrings with the thickest wire you can get through your pearls.

1. Cut the wire in two 3-inch (7.6 cm) pieces. Set aside.

2. Slide a pearl onto one of the wires and center it.

3. Holding the pearl in place, bend both wire ends around the tube until they cross (figure 1). Check that the pearl still sits in the center of the wire and that the wire ends are even.

fig. 1

4. Use chain-nose pliers to form a slight bend on each wire where the wires cross, or about ⅜ inch (9 mm) from each wire end (figure 2).

fig. 2

5. Form a simple loop at each wire end. Make sure the loops are the same size (figure 3). Use chain-nose pliers to squeeze the loops together so they sit next to each other. Set aside.

6. Use chain-nose pliers to grasp one of the ear wire's loops, right underneath the spot where the wire touches itself. Gently turn the loop 90°.

fig. 3

7. Attach the earring finding so it holds both simple loops.

8. Repeat steps 2 through 7 to make a second earring.

Nefertiti

These elegant earrings are worthy embellishments for a queen of the Nile. You can make a more understated version by making just one ring of pearls instead of four.

Designer: Sharon Bateman

Finished Size

1⅜ inches (3.4 cm)

Materials

48 freshwater pearls, 5-mm rice

48 gold-filled, 26-gauge headpins,
1 inch (2.5 cm) long

8 gold-filled, 8-mm jump rings
(or make your own from 5 inches
[12.7 cm] of gold-filled 20-gauge wire)

2 gold-filled earring findings

Tools

2 sets of chain-nose pliers

Round-nose pliers

Flush cutters, optional

¼-inch (6 mm) dowel, 4 inches
(10.2 cm) long, optional

Metal file or emery board, optional

Techniques

Wrapped loop (page 27)

Making jump rings (page 26), optional

Opening and closing rings (page 25)

Instructions

1. Slide one pearl onto a headpin. Make a wrapped loop to secure the pearl. Repeat to make 48 pearl dangles in all. Set aside.

2. If desired, make your own jump rings (see page 26).

3. Use the chain-nose pliers to open a jump ring. Slide on six pearl dangles and an earring finding. Close the jump ring.

4. Open a jump ring and slip six pearl dangles onto it. Before closing the jump ring, attach it to the jump ring from the previous step (figure 1).

fig. 1

5. Repeat step 4 until you've connected four pearl dangle-embellished jump rings.

6. Repeat all steps to make a second earring.

Shanghai
Click

The pearls in this pendant showcase a filigree button scavenged from a box of old family jewelry. The button may have come from Shanghai since the designer's great-grandparents lived there in the 1920s.

Designer: Nathalie Mornu

Finished Size

Pendant, 2⅛ inches (5.4 cm) long

Materials

25 freshwater pearls in various colors, 5- to 7-mm buttons and potatoes

2 sterling silver jump rings, 3.5 mm

1 sterling silver split ring, 5 mm

25 sterling silver head pins, 2 inches (5.1 cm) long

Vintage silver shank button, 16 x 18 mm

1½-inch (3.8 cm) length of 1.9-mm sterling silver chain

2½-foot (76.2 cm) length of 3.6 mm sterling silver long and short chain

Liver of sulfur (optional)

Tools

Plastic or glass container for liver of sulfur solution (optional)

Wire cutters

Chain-nose pliers

Round-nose pliers

Techniques

Wrapped loop (page 27)

Opening and closing rings (page 25)

Instructions

1. If desired, add a patina to the findings. Drop a pea-sized piece of liver of sulfur into a container and dissolve it with a half cup (11.8 cl) of boiling water. *Note:* Liver of sulfur is poisonous; don't handle it with bare hands, and don't employ a container or utensils that have been in contact with it for food use. Dip all the sterling silver findings in the solution to match the patina of the vintage button. Rinse the findings and let dry.

2. Use one 3.5-mm jump ring to attach the button's shank to one end of the shorter chain (figure 1).

fig. 1

3. Slide a 7-mm pearl onto a head pin. Form a wrapped loop that attaches to the short chain's end link (next to the button). Use the same method to attach another pearl to the other side of the link (figure 2). Skip a link and attach another pair of large pearls. Continue in this manner, working your way up the chain; use the largest pearls first, then the medium-sized ones, and finally the smallest ones. If you see gaps you find unattractive, add a pearl to fill it in. After you've used up all the pearls, cut off any extra chain, making sure to leave one empty link beyond the last pearl.

fig. 2

4. Use a 3.5-mm jump ring to attach the last link of the short chain to the split ring.

5. Attach each end of the long chain to the split ring.

Garland

This nature-inspired necklace looks like a dainty chain of flowers a wood fairy might fashion. Change the pearl, crystal, and metal types and you can evoke any season of the year.

Designer: Ellen Gerritse

Finished Size

16 inches (40.6 cm)

Materials

46 brown freshwater pearls, 6-mm half-round potato

22 transparent brown crystal bicones, 4 mm

22 size 11° transparent topaz seed beads

68 dark copper head pins, 1½ inches (3.8 cm)

68 dark copper crimp tubes, 2 x 2 mm

1 dark copper split ring, 5 mm

1 dark copper spring ring clasp, 8 mm

1-inch (2.5-cm) length of 4-mm twisted oval link dark copper chain

Tools

Crimping pliers

Wire cutters

Flat-nose pliers

Round-nose pliers

Ruler or measuring tape

Techniques

Crimping (page 28)

Simple loop (page 26)

Opening and closing rings (page 25)

Instructions

1. Slide a crimp tube onto a head pin. Snug the tube next to the pin's head and crimp. String on a pearl. Make a 90° bend in the wire 4 mm from the top of the pearl. Form a simple loop starting at the bend. Open the loop and attach it to an end link on the chain. Set this chain extender aside.

2. String a crimp tube onto a head pin. Snug the tube up to the pin's head and crimp. Slide on a pearl. As in step 1, measure 4 mm from the top of the pearl, bend the wire 90° then make a simple loop. Finish the loop and attach it to the clasp. Set aside.

3. Slide a crimp tube onto a head pin. Push the tube snugly beside the pin's head and crimp. String on a pearl. As before, make a simple loop 4 mm from the top of the pearl. Open the loop and attach it to the head pin made in step 2, between the pearl and the clasp (figure 1). Set aside.

fig. 1

4. String a crimp tube onto a head pin. Snug the tube next to the pin's head and crimp. String on one seed bead and one crystal. Make a simple loop 4 mm from the top of the crystal. Open the loop and attach it to the head pin added in the previous step, between the bead and the simple loop.

5. Slide a crimp tube onto a head pin. Push the tube snugly next to the pin's head and crimp. String on a pearl. Make a simple loop 4 mm from the top of the crystal. Open the loop and attach it to the head pin added in the previous step, between the bead and the simple loop.

Designer's Tip

Marking the jaws of your flat-nose pliers to 4 mm will speed the process of making the necklace.

6. Repeat step 5.

7. Repeat steps 4 through 6 twenty times.

8. Repeat step 4. Set the necklace aside.

9. Cut the head off of a head pin. Make a simple loop at one end. Use the split ring to attach the loop and the open end of the chain. String on a crimp tube, snug it next to the loop, and crimp. String on a pearl and make a simple loop 4 mm from the first simple loop. Attach this loop to the head pin added in step 8, between the bead and the simple loop (figure 2).

fig. 2

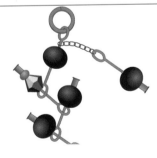

Blueprint

A combination of techniques—light metalsmithing, ink stamping, and wirework—makes this a fun project to create. The resulting earrings are stylish, with a bohemian flair.

Designer: Andrea McLester

Finished Size

1¾ inches (4.5 cm) long

Materials

2 dark blue freshwater pearls,
17-mm peanut

2 sterling silver 22-gauge, ball-end
head pins, 2 inches (5.1 cm) long

24-gauge sterling silver sheet, at least
1½ x 2½ inches (3.8 x 6.4 cm)

12-inch (30.5 cm) length of 20-gauge
sterling silver wire

Midnight blue permanent ink stamp
pad (ink should be able to adhere
to metal)

Water-based dimensional
adhesive glaze

Isopropyl alcohol

Cotton balls

Instructions

1. Wrap the 20-gauge wire around the dowel to make two complete coils. Slide the coils off the dowel, and cut the wire so you have two identical rings (figure 1). Set the rings aside.

fig. 1

2. Cut the silver sheet into two ¾ x 1¼-inch (1.9 x 3.2 cm) pieces. Take care not to scratch the metal as you handle it. Clean each piece with silver polish to remove any tarnish, ink, or other residue. File any sharp edges and round each corner slightly. Set the tags aside.

3. Put the paper on a flat, clean, level surface and place one of the tags on top. Press your stamp on the ink pad, and immediately press the inked stamp onto the tag. Be careful not to smear the design as you lift the stamp, but if you do, simply moisten a cotton ball with isopropyl alcohol and wipe off the ink. Once the tag has dried, re-stamp. Let the ink dry for one hour.

4. Use the brush to apply a thick layer of glaze to the tag, covering the entire printed area. Don't let the glaze ooze over the tag's edge. Inspect the surface for bubbles and eliminate any by poking them with a straight pin. Let it dry completely.

5. Use the marker to make a small dot on the tag 2 mm from the top center.

6. Place the tag, plain side down, on the piece of wood. If you have a drill press available, set the drill into it (the press makes for precision drilling). Put on the safety glasses. Turn on the drill and lower the end of the bit directly onto the dot, keeping the drill perpendicular to the tag. Once drilled through, file the back of the tag smooth. Set the tag aside.

7. Slip a pearl onto a head pin. Make a wrapped loop to secure the pearl. Set the pearl dangle aside.

8. Form a simple loop at one end of one of the rings. Use chain-nose pliers to bend the loop at a 90° angle perpendicular to the wire.

9. Use chain-nose pliers to straighten the other end of the wire for ⅝ inch (1.6 cm) so it will fit through an earlobe. File any burrs. Use your fingers to shape the ear wire, allowing the straightened end to pass through the loop (figure 2).

fig. 2

10. Use the straightened end of the ear wire to string on the tag, back to front, and the pearl dangle. Close the ear wire.

11. Repeat steps 3 through 10 to make a second earring.

Tools

Jeweler's saw or tin snips

Polishing cloth

Metal file, sandpaper, or coarse emery board

Sheet of paper

Rubber stamp

Small craft brush

Straight pin

Fine-point permanent marker

Piece of scrap wood

Safety glasses

Drill (twist or electric) with 1-mm bit

Drill press (optional)

Chain-nose pliers

Round-nose pliers

Flush cutters

Needle-nose pliers (preferably smooth-jawed)

1-inch (2.5 cm) diameter wooden dowel, 4 inches (10.2 cm) long

Techniques

Coiling wire (page 24)

Simple loop (page 26)

Wrapped loop (page 27)

Siren's Song

A mixture of pearls, crystals, and sterling silver evokes an underwater symphony. This necklace uses simple stringing techniques. End cones hide the knots that keep the strands together.

Designer: Ellen Gerritse

Finished Size

19¾ inches (50.2 cm)

Materials

49 silver freshwater pearls, 8-mm potato

99 black freshwater pearls, 6-mm potato

90 black freshwater pearls, 3-mm potato

98 opal crystals in bicone and round shapes, 4 mm

49 sterling silver-plated curved and twisted tubes, 2 x 24 mm

204 sterling silver-plated seamless rounds, 2 mm and 3 mm

2 sterling silver seamless cones, 15 mm

1 sterling silver round box clasp with ivory pearl inlay, 10 mm

Dark gray silk beading thread

Clear glue

Tools

Scissors

7 English beading needles, size 12 or 13

Techniques

Knotting (page 29)

Instructions

1. Cut a 28-inch (71.1 cm) length of thread. Make a square knot about 4 inches (10.2 cm) from one end. Thread it on a needle. String on beads in the following sequence to make the first strand: One 3-mm pearl, one tube, one 3-mm pearl, one seamless round, one crystal, one 6-mm pearl, one seamless round, one 8-mm pearl, one seamless round, one 6-mm pearl, one crystal, one seamless round, and one 3-mm pearl. Repeat this sequence six more times. Snug the beads against the knot and set the strand aside with the needle still attached.

2. Repeat step 1 six more times to make a total of seven strands.

3. Place two of the strands together and make an overhand knot at the top of the last beads strung. Pair the needles together and pass both needles through one seamless round. Repeat with two more strands. Knot the four strands together (figure 1).

fig. 1

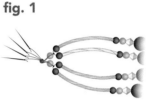

4. Knot the remaining three strands together as you did in step 3. Gather the needles together and string on two seamless rounds. Place this set of three strands next to the set of four strands on the work surface. Arrange the strands so the first beads strung on the four-strand set are next to the last beads strung on the three-strand set. Weave the set of three strands loosely through the set of four to create a twisted effect. Group the ends of the three strands together and make a knot. Gather the needles together and string on one seamless round. Remove the needles from one end of the three-strand set and thread them on the other end.

5. Gather all seven strands and knot them together at each end, taking care to avoid leaving any slack in the thread. Pass the strands with the needles on them through one cone and one half of the clasp. Pass back through the cone, pull tight, and make two knots (figure 2). Glue the knots to secure. After they dry completely, trim any excess thread.

6. Thread the needles on the other end of the strands. Repeat step 5 on the other end of the necklace, being careful to hide the knots inside the cone.

fig. 2

Flapper Chain

It's not tricky work to create this versatile necklace. Wear it long and open, flapper style; tie one end in a loose overhand knot to make a faux pendant; or double it around your neck for a princess-length contemporary look.

Flapper Chain

Designer: Nathalie Mornu

Finished Size

39 inches (99.1 cm)

Materials

7 violet crystals in varying shapes and finishes, 6 to 8 mm

12 violet pearls, 7-mm potato

1 gunmetal split ring, 3.5 mm

1 gunmetal split ring, 5 mm

7 gunmetal split rings, 6 mm

30-inch (76.2 cm) length of 1.9-mm link gunmetal chain

26-gauge silver craft wire, 4 feet (1.2 m) long

Liver of sulfur

Tools

Plastic or glass container for liver of sulfur solution

Wire cutters

Chain-nose pliers

Round-nose pliers

Techniques

Wrapped loop (page 27)

Instructions

1. Drop a pea-size piece of liver of sulfur into a container and dissolve it with a half cup (11.8 cl) of boiling water. *Note:* Liver of sulfur is poisonous; don't handle it with bare hands, and don't employ a container or utensils that have been or will be used in preparing food. Gently form the wire so it fits into the container and place it in the solution until it has a patina that matches the color of the chain. Remove the wire, then rinse and dry it.

2. Cut the chain into 25 pieces of different lengths, none less than ¾ inch (1.9 cm) long. Set aside.

3. Cut a 1½-inch (3.8 cm) piece of wire and make a small wrapped loop at one end, but before you make the wrap, attach the loop to the end link of one of the chain pieces. String one of the beads onto the same wire and make another small wrapped loop at the other end of the wire that attaches to the end of another chain piece (figure 1).

    fig. 1

    Connect the other end of this chain piece to a split ring. Repeat to create a random strand of beaded links, chain, and split rings. For three of the beaded links use two pearls instead of one (figure 2).

    fig. 2

4. Attach the last beaded link to the open end of the first chain piece to close the strand into a necklace.

Simple Pleasures

A chunky button is the star of this understated bracelet.
Besides being a focal element, it serves as half of the closure.

Designer: Debra Saldivar

Finished Size

10¼ inches (26 cm)

Materials

11 blue iris freshwater pearls, 7-mm potato

10 ivory freshwater pearls, 8-mm top-drilled potato

Approximately 82 midnight blue cylinder beads, regular (comparable to size 11° seed beads)

4 sterling silver Bali-style barrels, 12 x 16 mm

1 sterling silver seamless round, 3 mm

1 sterling silver 24-gauge head pin, 2 inches (5.1 cm)

2 sterling silver crimp tubes, 2 x 2 mm

1 horn two-holed button, 3.2 cm

20-inch (50.8 cm) length of fine, flexible beading wire

Tools

Round-nose pliers

Chain-nose pliers

Wire cutters

Clip or bead stopper

Crimping pliers

Techniques

Wrapped loop (page 27)

Crimping (page 28)

Instructions

Note: If you require a smaller bracelet size, simply reduce the number or size of beads for the final design.

1. Slide a blue pearl onto the head pin. Make a wrapped loop with a ⅛-inch (3 mm) loop. Set the dangle aside.

2. Place a clip at one end of the beading wire. String on four cylinder beads, one crimp tube, and 20 cylinder beads. Pass the wire up through one hole of the button from back to front. String on the dangle created in the previous step so it slides over the cylinder beads. Pass down through the other hole of the button from front to back. Pass back through the crimp tube and the first four cylinder beads strung in this step so you have a ½-inch (1.3 cm) wire tail exiting the last bead (figure 1). Snug the beads and crimp the tube. Trim the excess tail wire. Remove the clip.

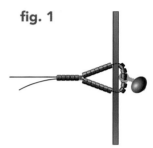

fig. 1

3. String on a sequence of one blue pearl and one cylinder bead four times. String on one blue pearl and one silver barrel. String on five ivory pearls and one silver barrel. Repeat this step.

4. String on one seamless round, one crimp tube, and approximately 58 cylinder beads, or enough that when made into a loop the beads fit snugly over the button. Pass back through the crimp tube, seamless round, and barrel bead to make a loop (figure 2). Snug the beads and crimp the tube. Trim any excess wire close to the beads.

fig. 2

Spiral Axis

Individually, the spiral dangles in this project appear somewhat plain, but fill a handmade chain with them and you end up with a stunning piece that's runway-worthy.

Designer: Elizabeth Larsen

Finished Size

8¼ inches (21 cm)

Materials

24 lavender freshwater pearls, 5-mm to 6-mm half-round potato

13 purple freshwater pearls, 5- to 6-mm oval

76 violet crystal rounds, 6 mm

15 light amethyst crystal rounds, 6 mm

1 sterling silver and marcasite toggle clasp, 19 mm

5-foot (1.5 m) length of 20-gauge, full- or half-hard, sterling silver wire

32-foot (9.8 m) length of 24-gauge, full- or half-hard, sterling silver wire

Jeweler's cement adhesive

Tools

Flush cutters

Flat-nose pliers

Chain-nose pliers

Round-nose pliers

2.75-mm (size 2 US) knitting needle

Techniques

Wrapped loop (page 27)

Jump rings (page 25)

Instructions

Note: The materials are for a 6¾-inch to 7-inch (17.2 cm to 17.9 cm) wrist. Add or subtract materials to make a larger or smaller bracelet.

1. Tightly coil the 20-gauge wire around the knitting needle down the needle's length. Slide the end of the coil off the end of the needle. Cut the coils one at a time to make jump rings. Make 130 jump rings in all.

2. Open two jump rings. Connect the two rings to two closed (stacked) jump rings. Repeat to make a chain 64 links long (figure 1).

fig. 1

You should have two jump rings left over. Use one to connect one half of the clasp to one end of the chain. Repeat at the other end. Set the chain aside.

3. Cut a 3-inch (7.6 cm) piece of 24-gauge wire. Form a wrapped loop at one end of the wire. String on a pearl and form a second wrapped loop, but don't cut the wire.

4. Hold the second loop with a pair of flat-nose pliers. Use chain-nose pliers to wrap the wire around and down the body of the bead until the wire meets the first loop. Loosely wrap the wire end around the first loop's base, and use chain-nose pliers to tighten the wrap (figure 2). Secure the wire end by adding a dab of adhesive where you've made the wrap. Repeat with each bead to make a total of 128 dangles. Set them aside.

fig. 2

5. Lay the dangles on the work surface in the following sequence: One lavender pearl, four violet crystals, one light amethyst crystal, one lavender pearl, two violet crystals, and one purple pearl. Repeat the sequence until you've arranged all the dangles.

6. Carefully open the second set of links at one end of the bracelet without dismantling the chain. Attach the first lavender pearl dangle. Slide the links around so they open at the other side of the chain and attach the next dangle in the sequence from step 5 (the first violet crystal). You should end up with one dangle on each side of the chain (figure 3).

    fig. 3

    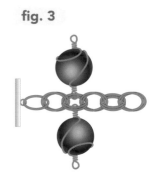

7. Continue to add dangles down the length of the chain, following the sequence from step 5, until you reach the other end. The placement of dangles may be adjusted so there aren't too many of one kind of bead on one side of the bracelet.

Bronze Drops

A single Tahitian pearl, showcased in a handmade open spiral cap, hangs amidst clusters of smaller pearls. The setting allows the pearl's natural shape, magnificent luster, and color variations to shine.

Designer: Sandra Lupo

Finished Size

18 inches (45.7 cm)

Materials

1 dark green Tahitian pearl, 10 x 14-mm teardrop, un-drilled or half-drilled

12 peridot freshwater pearls, 4-mm buttons

6 dark gray freshwater pearls, 4-mm rounds

12 light gray freshwater pearls, 3-mm rounds

12 semiprecious peridot faceted rondelles, 4 mm

24 gold-filled head pins, 1 inch (2.1 cm) long

6 gold-filled 22-gauge jump rings, 4 x 5-mm ovals

1 gold-filled toggle clasp, 6 mm

16-inch (40.6 cm) length of 4-mm oval twist link gold-filled chain, or desired length

12-inch (30.5 cm) length of manufactured twist wire, or 2-foot (61 cm) length of 24-gauge, soft, gold-filled wire

Two-part 5-minute epoxy glue

Instructions

1. Slide two peridot pearls onto a head pin. Make a simple loop to secure the pearls. Repeat with all of the peridot pearls to make six bead dangles in all. Continue creating bead dangles in this fashion, making six using two light gray pearls each; six using two semiprecious peridot beads each; and six using one dark gray pearl each. Set the 24 bead dangles aside.

2. If you need to make your own twisted wire, fold the 24-gauge wire in half and place each of the wire ends into the chuck of the wire twister or pin vise. Stabilize the looped wire end by clamping it onto a table or other surface (figure 1). Turn the reel of the twister or pin vise in one direction until you are pleased with the level of twist. *Note:* The tighter you twist wire, the harder it will become, making it more difficult to work with later. You may want to experiment with a length of copper or brass wire first to find the optimum twist level. Remove the wire from the twister and clamp and trim each wire end. You should end up with about 10 inches (25.4 cm) of twisted wire.

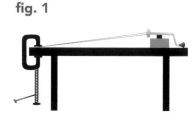

fig. 1

3. Use the chain-nose pliers to make a ¼-inch (6 mm) right-angle bend at the end of the wire and form a three-coil wrapped loop at the bend. When you turn the loop, make it 3 to 4 mm in diameter. *Note:* There will be a short stem of wire below the wrapped loop. Don't trim it—you will use this to attach the large pearl.

4. Use the long end of the wire to form a spiral that fits over the top of the pearl, creating a wire bead cap (figure 2). Use the top of the pearl as your guide, but take care not to mar the pearl's nacre. Pull the spiral slightly apart so it forms to the pearl's shape.

fig. 2

5. Once you achieve the desired shape, trim the long wire but leave a ¼-inch (6 mm) excess. File the wire end smooth. Use the tip of round-nose pliers to form a small loop at the wire's end.

Tools

Chain-nose pliers

Round-nose pliers

Flush cutters

Wire twister and clamp or pin vise (unnecessary if manufactured wire is used)

Needle file or emery board

Pearl holder

Fine-point permanent marker

Small drill and 1-mm chisel drill bit (if using an undrilled pearl)

Techniques

Simple loop (page 26)

Wrapped loop (page 27)

Wire spiral (page 25)

6. If necessary, drill a small vertical hole at the top of the pearl. Place the pearl vertically, top side up, into the pearl holder to keep it stable. Mark the place where you want to drill. Drill into that mark until you reach one-third of the way down the pearl's center. *Note:* It may help to keep a small amount of cool water nearby to wet the drill bit, keeping it and the pearl cool during drilling. Let the pearl dry, blow out any excess dust, and set aside.

7. Use a small amount of epoxy to thoroughly coat the spiral cap's straight wire. Fit the wire into the pearl (figure 3). Use a cushioned support or clamp to hold the pearl and cap in place while the epoxy dries.

fig. 3

8. Use two jump rings to attach the pendant's loop to a link at the center of the chain.

9. Count four links down one side of the chain from the link to which you added the pendant. Add one of each type of bead dangle to this link. Count four more links down the chain and add another four bead dangles. Repeat one more time so you have three bead clusters in all. Repeat this step down the chain on the other side of the pendant.

10. Use two jump rings to attach one half of the clasp to one end of the chain. Repeat at the other end of the chain.

Intermediate
PROJECTS

Baroque Loops

This versatile pendant would look as pretty incorporated into an elaborate necklace as it would on a simple gold chain. Even if you're unfamiliar with wireworking, you're sure to garner beautiful results.

Finished Size

¾ x 1½ inches (20 x 40 mm)

Materials

1 mabe pearl cabochon, 18 x 27 mm

Surrounding wires: 25-inch (63.5 cm) length of 22-gauge, dead-soft, round, 14-karat gold-filled wire 10-inch (25.4 cm) length of 22-gauge, half-hard, round, 14-karat gold-filled wire

Wrapping wire: 10-inch (25.4 cm) length of 22-gauge, half-hard, half-round, 14-karat gold-filled wire

Tools

Flexible tape measure

Safety glasses

Flush cutters

Polishing cloth

Non-serrated flat-nose pliers (with spring)

Non-serrated chain-nose pliers

Flexible straightedge ruler

¼-inch (6 mm) wooden dowel, 4 inches (10.2 cm) long

Needle-nose pliers

Leather mallet

Techniques

Coiling wire (page 24)

Wire spiral (page 25)

Instructions

1. Measure the perimeter of the pearl and add 6 inches (15.2 cm). Put on the safety glasses and cut two pieces of dead-soft round wire and one piece of half-hard round wire to that length. These are called the "surrounding wires." Cut one 5-inch (12.7 cm) piece of dead-soft round wire. Straighten each wire by pulling it between your fingers or through the polishing cloth.

2. Straighten the half-round "wrapping wire" by pulling it between your fingers or through the polishing cloth. Use flat- or chain-nose pliers to bend the end of the wrapping wire ¼ inch (6 mm) from the end to make a hook. The curved side of the wire should be on the outside of the hook.

3. Hold the three surrounding wires side by side, the half-hard wire between the dead-soft wires. Position the center of the wires at the bottom of the pearl and use your fingers to begin to gently shape the wires up along the side of the pearl.

4. Set the pearl aside, but imagine it as a clock face. While holding the surrounding wires between your thumb and index fingers, place the wrapping wire's hook (created in step 2) on the surrounding wires at the equivalent of the five o'clock position on the pearl's face. Keep the short end of the wrapping wire on the outside of the surrounding wires, away from where the pearl will sit. Coil the wrapping wire tightly around the three surrounding wires a few times (figure 1).

fig. 1

5. Gently squeeze the coil with flat-nose pliers to flatten the wraps and make sure they're uniform. Continue coiling the wrapping wire until you've completed about fifteen wraps, or until you reach the equivalent of seven o'clock on the pearl's face. As you coil the wire, ensure that each wrap is even and tight. Trim the wrapping wire to ¼ inch (6 mm) from the surrounding wires. Use flat-nose pliers to tuck the wrapping wire under the surrounding wires. Tuck the other end of the wrapping

wire under the surrounding wires. Trim each end to the same length so each side is uniform. Use flat- or chain-nose pliers to squeeze the wrapping wire more vigorously, tightening it around the surrounding wires (figure 2).

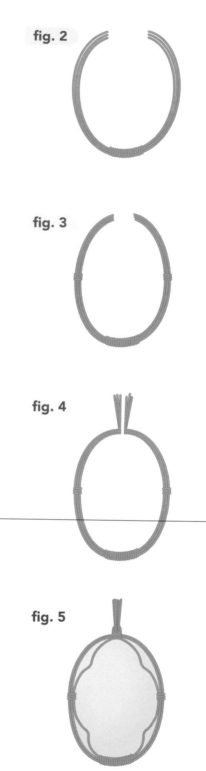

fig. 2

6. Repeat step 2 with the remaining wrapping wire. Continue to shape the surrounding wires up the side of the pearl. Place this hook at the equivalent of nine o'clock on the pearl's face. Coil the wrapping wire three times around the surrounding wires. Repeat this step to create a coil at three o'clock (figure 3). To make sure the side coils are positioned correctly, lay the straightedge ruler across the top edges of each side coil. Adjust the coils as necessary, and then use flat-nose pliers to vigorously tighten the coils.

fig. 3

7. Use your fingers to shape the surrounding wires around the pearl until they reach the top. When the wires meet, use flat-nose pliers to bend them directly up from the top of the pearl. The wires should be completely vertical and parallel to each other, creating a wire stem (figure 4).

8. Bend the remaining 5 inches (12.7 cm) of round, dead-soft wire in half around your finger. Hold the wire stem around the top of the pearl, and coil the wrap wire around it once. Use the chain- and flat-nose pliers to pull the wire ends in opposite directions, tightening the wrap.

fig. 4

9. Use chain-nose pliers to grasp the front surrounding wire underneath the nine o'clock coil. Make a slight kink in the wire, pulling up toward the coil while you keep the wire in place with your forefinger. Repeat with the same surrounding wire, this time above the nine o'clock coil and making the kink down toward the coil. Repeat this step for the three o'clock coil, making sure to use the front surrounding wire (figure 5).

fig. 5

10. Place the wire frame over the front of the pearl. Push the wire frame gently around the top side of the pearl, then turn it over. Use chain-nose pliers to repeat step 9 with the back surrounding wire, encasing the pearl. *Note:* If the pearl slips out of the frame at the bottom, gently pull up on the front surrounding wire on either side just above the bottom wrap wire, being careful not to put a kink in the wire.

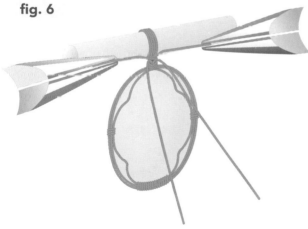

fig. 6

11. Coil the 5-inch (12.7 cm) dead-soft round wire two more times down the stem. Use flat-nose pliers to tighten the coil. Trim the wire ends so they're at the back of the pendant.

12. Bend the two front surrounding wires down over the front of the pearl. Bend the two back surrounding wires down over the back of the pearl.

13. Straighten the center wires so they point straight up from the top of the pendant. Hold the wooden dowel in front of the center wires and make two tight forward coils around the dowel with each wire. The loops should be on either side of the pendant's center. Grasp the wire ends with chain- and flat-nose pliers and crisscross them along the back of the pendant, tightening them to the center (figure 6). One wire will be on top of the other. Pull the top wire up and out of the way. Use flat-nose pliers to wrap the bottom wire once around all the stem wires at the top of the coil. Trim the wire so it sits at the back of the pendant and use chain-nose pliers to tuck the end into the stem. Repeat with the top wire, making the wrap in the opposite direction.

14. Trim the two back surrounding wires to ¼ inch (6 mm). Form a small spiral and bend it down and flat against the back of the pearl to hide the stem. Repeat with the other back surrounding wire and bend it up and flat against the back of the stem.

15. Trim the top left surrounding wire to 1¼ inches (3.2 cm) and the bottom right one to ¾ inch (1.9 cm). Form and place spirals as in step 14, bending the larger spiral down and the smaller spiral up over the front of the pendant. Use flat-nose pliers to gently squeeze all of the coils into place.

16. With the dowel still in place, gently tap the bail coils about four times to harden the wire. Holding the pendant in one hand, gently but firmly twist the dowel back and forth until you work it out of the bail.

Golden Crescent

Wire and pearls are the only materials required to make these delicate earrings. They are each made similarly but can be shaped differently to create extra asymmetrical interest.

Designer: Cynthia B. Wuller

Finished Size

1¾ inches (4.4 cm) long

Materials

2 white freshwater pearls, 4-mm half-round potato

2 gold-filled earring findings

9-inch (22.9 cm) length of 20-gauge, dead-soft, gold-filled wire

4-inch (10.2 cm) length of 24-gauge, dead-soft, gold-filled wire

Tools

Wire cutters

Ruler

2 chain-nose pliers

Round-nose pliers

Chasing hammer

Bench block

Techniques

Coiling wire (page 24)

Simple loop (page 26)

Opening and closing rings (page 25)

Instructions

1. Cut two 4¼-inch (10.8 cm) pieces of 20-gauge wire. Cut two 2-inch (5.1 cm) pieces of 24-gauge wire. Set aside.

2. Use chain-nose pliers to bend one piece of 20-gauge wire into a slightly off-center *V* shape. Shape one side of the wire by pinching it between your thumb and forefinger and pulling down to slightly curve the wire. Repeat on the other side of the *V* so you end up with a leaf-like shape.

3. Use one pair of chain-nose pliers to make a 90° bend ⅜ inch (9 mm) from the end of the long side of the wire. The bend should point away from the center of the wire shape. Use one pair of chain-nose pliers to make a slight bend ⅜ inch (9 mm) from the end of the short side of the wire so it sticks straight up from the shape, perpendicular to the 90° bend (figure 1).

   fig. 1

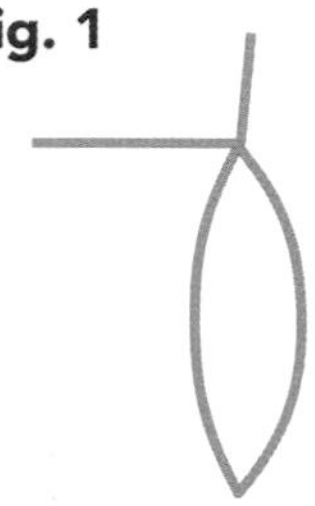

4. Use one pair of chain-nose pliers to grasp the wires tightly just below where they cross. Use the second pair of chain-nose pliers to wrap the 90° bent wire tightly around the straight wire twice to create a coil. Trim the wrapping wire and use chain-nose pliers to squeeze the tail close to the coil. Form a simple loop on the other wire end (figure 2)

   fig. 2

5. Use your fingers to gently push the shorter side of the wire shape toward the longer side, making it concave. Pull the widest part of the curve on the longer side of the wire shape, expanding it. Use chain-nose pliers to straighten any kinks. Continue refining the wire shape with your fingers and the pliers until you are pleased with its appearance.

fig. 3

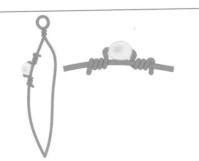

6. Hammer the wire shape (not the coiled and looped section) on the bench block to flatten the wire and create texture.

7. Use chain-nose pliers to bend a sharp angle ½ inch (1.3 cm) from the end of a 2-inch (5.2 cm) piece of 24-gauge wire. Place the bent wire over the widest curve on the longer side of the wire shape. Use your thumb and forefinger to hold the bent wire in place as you wrap the wire tail around the wire shape twice, making a tight coil. Use chain-nose pliers to tighten and squeeze the coil. Wrap one more time, tightening and squeezing as before.

8. Use the tip of the chain-nose pliers to bend the wrapping wire so it's perpendicular to the wire shape. Estimate the height of the bead from hole-to-hole and bend the wire so it's parallel to the wire shape. String on one pearl so the flat side touches the wire. Make three tight coils around the wire shape, just below the pearl. Slide the pearl to where it looks best on the curve. Use chain-nose pliers to tighten the coil and make one more wrap (figure 3). Trim the wrapping wire ends on the back side of the wire and use chain-nose pliers to squeeze the tails close to the wraps. Use chain-nose pliers to firmly grasp and flatten the wrapped wire. Squeeze the coils back together if they spread apart.

9. Attach an ear wire to the simple loop.

10. Repeat steps 2 through 9 to make a second earring. The shapes should be similar, but they don't need to be identical; the second pearl can be placed anywhere on the long side of the second earring.

Whirlwind

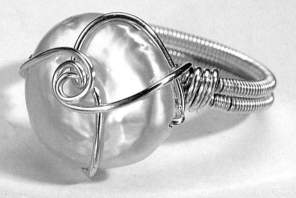

This stunning cocktail ring features a whorl of silver wire on top. Shape the design as shown, or give it your own style by experimenting with twisting the wire.

Whirlwind

Designer: Marie Lee Carter

Finished Size

Ring top, 5/16 x 5/8 inches (8 x 16 mm)

Materials

1 white freshwater pearl, 14-mm coin

16-inch (40.6 cm) length of 18- or 20-gauge round sterling silver wire (whichever will fit through the pearl's hole)

30-inch (76.2 cm) length of 24- or 26-gauge round sterling silver wire

Tools

Tape measure

Flush cutters

Bead reamer (optional)

Flat-nose pliers

Metal file

Ring mandrel

Plastic mallet

Tumbler with stainless steel shot or plastic pellets and dishwashing liquid

Techniques

Coiling wire (page 24)

Instructions

1. Measure and cut a 16-inch (40.6 cm) length of 18- or 20-gauge wire. *Note:* If you wish to use the thicker gauge for a more substantial look, use a bead reamer to increase the size of the pearl's hole.

2. Use flat-nose pliers to make a 90° bend about halfway down the wire. String on the pearl and slide it to the bend. Make another 90° bend on the other side of the pearl. Use flat-nose pliers to grasp the wire ¼ inch (6 mm) from the 90° bend on one side of the pearl. Make a 45° bend away from the pearl to secure it. Make another 45° bend on the other side of the pearl (figure 1). Arrange the wire—now called the "base wire"—so it sticks straight out from the sides of the pearl.

   fig. 1

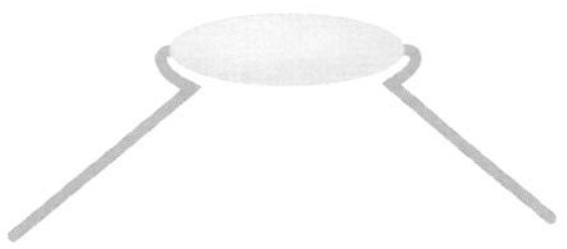

   fig. 2

3. Working on one side of the pearl, use your fingers or flat-nose pliers and the 24- or 26-gauge wire to make a tight 2- to 2½-inch (5.1 to 6.4 cm) coil (depending on your desired ring size) around the heavier wire. Check your wraps for uniformity and neatness. Trim the first end of the wrapping wire close to the base wire and push the coil up to one of the 45° bends (figure 2). File any sharp edges. Repeat this step on the other side of the pearl.

   fig. 3

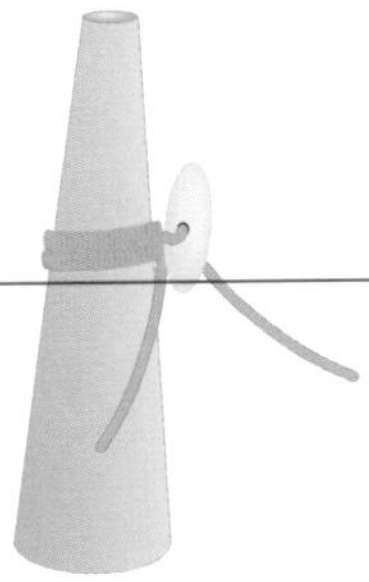

4. Place the piece on the mandrel at a half size larger than your desired final size. Use your index finger and thumb to firmly press one of the wrapped base wires around the mandrel to create the ring's shank. Wrap the other wrapped base wire around the mandrel in the other direction, creating a double wire shank (figure 3). Trim the wrapping wire ends as close to the base of the pearl as possible. Use flat-nose pliers to gently squeeze the wire tails close to the base and file any rough edges.

5. Wrap one of the bare base wires once around the opposite 45° bend at the base of the ring (figure 4). Repeat for the other bare base wire, wrapping it in the opposite direction. Bring each wire up and over the top of the pearl. Cross the two wires and create a swirl by winding the wires in a circle twice. Straighten the wires so they point in opposite directions on each side of the pearl (figure 5).

6. Bring one base wire down to the shank, right next to the pearl, and tightly coil it three and a half times around each wrapped base wire. Trim the base wire so it sits inside the ring and use flat-nose pliers to squeeze the tail close to the shank. File any rough edges. Repeat on the other side of the ring.

7. With the ring still on the mandrel, use the hammer to gently tap the shank all around to harden the wire.

8. Tumble the ring for 20 minutes.

fig. 4

fig. 5

Moon Glow

What seems an elaborate wireworking technique is simply extended wraps around a beaded wire stem. The result is an earring that evokes light emanating from a full moon.

Designer: Diana Light

Finished Size

1⅛ inches (2.8 cm)

Materials

2 cream freshwater pearls,
6-mm half-round

2 semiprecious citrine saucers, 4.5 mm

2 sterling silver lever-back
earring findings

20-inch (50.8 cm) length of 24-gauge,
soft sterling wire

Tools

Flush cutters

Ruler

Chain-nose pliers

Round-nose pliers

Techniques

Simple loop (page 26)

Coiling wire (page 24)

Instructions

1. Cut 2 inches (5.1 cm) of wire. Form a simple loop ½ inch (1.3 cm) from one end. Use chain-nose pliers to bend the wire's tail so it's parallel with the long wire end (figure 1).

2. Slide a citrine bead onto the open end of the wire from step 1. Pull the wire end up toward the loop and make a tight coil around the loop's base. Trim any excess wire (figure 2). Set this dangle aside.

3. Cut 2 inches (5.1 cm) of wire and make a wrapped loop that attaches to one of the ear wires.

4. Slide a pearl onto the open end of the wire from step 1. Measure ⅝ inch (1.6 cm) down from the wrapped loop and make another wrapped loop, this time attaching it to the dangle's loop (figure 3). Set this shank aside.

5. Cut 6 inches (15.2 cm) of wire. Hold the pearl halfway up the shank and use one end of the 6-inch (15.2 cm) piece to make one wrap just above the pearl. Trim the excess tail wire.

6. Keep the wire as close as possible to the pearl as you bring the wire down along one side of the pearl's perimeter. Make a wrap just below the pearl by crossing over the front of the wire shank, around the back to the front, and then back up the other side of the pearl's perimeter. Make another wrap above the last wrap on top of the pearl. As with the bottom wrap, cross over the front of the shank, around back, to the front, and down the side of the pearl (figure 4).

7. Repeat step 6 until you reach the wrapped loops at each end of the shank. Trim the excess wire and use chain-nose pliers to squeeze the tail, tucking it beneath the coil close to the wrap.

8. Repeat steps 1 through 7 to make the second earring.

fig. 1

fig. 2

fig. 3

fig. 4

Cocktail Hour

For this elegant bracelet, you'll weave a combination of coin pearls, crystals, and silver spacers using ladder stitch. When you're finished, the coin shapes will lie like fallen dominoes.

Designer: Sandra Lupo

Finished Size

8 inches (20.3 cm)

Materials

13 to 14 white freshwater pearls, 13-mm coin

1 white freshwater pearl bead, 8-mm round

72 clear crystal rounds, 4 mm

100 opaque white cylinder beads, regular size (compares to size 11°)

33 sterling silver spacers, 4-mm flat square

2 sterling silver 2 x 2-mm crimp beads

1 sterling silver crimp cover, 4 mm

45-inch (1.1 m) length of .012 silver-plated 19-strand flexible beading wire

Tools

Wire cutters (for cutting flexible wire)

Crimping pliers

Chain-nose pliers

Techniques

Ladder stitch (page 30)

Crimping (page 28)

Instructions

1. Cut 45 inches (1.1 m) of wire. String on the round pearl and slide it to the middle of the wire.

2. Pair the wire ends and string on one crystal, one spacer, and one crystal.

3. Separate the wire ends. On one, string on two cylinder beads, one crystal, one spacer, one crystal, and two cylinder beads. Repeat the stringing sequence for the other wire. String a coin onto one wire, and pass the other wire through the coin in the opposite direction (figure 1). Tighten the wires so all the beads are snug.

fig. 1

4. On one wire, string on one cylinder bead, one crystal, one spacer, one crystal, and one cylinder bead. Repeat the stringing sequence for the other wire. Use one wire to string on one coin and pass the other wire through the coin in the opposite direction. Tighten the wires to snug the beads.

5. Repeat step 4 until you are about ¾ inch (1.9 cm) from your desired size.

6. On one wire, string one cylinder bead, one crystal, one spacer, one crystal, and two cylinder beads. Repeat the stringing sequence for the other wire. Pair the wires and string on one crystal, one crimp bead, one crystal, one crimp bead, and 24 cylinder beads. Snug all the beads.

7. Hold the last cylinder bead strung so it sits tightly above the last crimp bead strung. Check to see that this loop fits snugly over the round pearl and make adjustments as necessary. Pass the wires back through the last crimp bead strung, the next crystal, the first crimp bead strung, and the next crystal (figure 2). Crimp the crimp beads and trim the wire close to the work. Add a crimp cover over the crimp nestled between the two crystals at this end of the bracelet.

fig. 2

Abundance

A wide variety of pearls embellishes this free-form crocheted necklace. The delicate wire and subtle array of white hues make it a perfect necklace for a wedding or any other formal occasion.

Abundance

Designer: Mirtha Aertker

Finished Size

17½ inches (44.5 cm)

Materials

12 ivory/light gray freshwater pearls, 18-mm stick

1 ivory Majorca pearl, 15-mm round

1 white freshwater pearl, 14-mm diamond

2 peacock freshwater pearls, 10-mm flat square

6 ivory Majorca glass pearls, 9-mm round

4 ivory Majorca glass pearls, 7-mm round

18 light gray freshwater pearls, 6-mm potato

75 white freshwater pearls, 4-mm potato

20 white freshwater pearls, 4-mm button

2 to 6 sterling silver crimp beads (optional)

1 sterling silver box clasp with marcasite 15-mm round

3 spools of 28-gauge silver craft wire, each 25 feet (7.6 m) long

2 spools of 32-gauge silver craft wire, each 25 feet (7.6 m) long

Instructions

1. String an assortment of pearls onto one spool of 28-gauge wire in the following sequence: One 4-mm button, one 7-mm Majorca, one gray potato, one square, one gray potato, one 9-mm Majorca, one gray potato, one 9-mm Majorca, one gray potato, one 9-mm Majorca, and one gray potato. String on one 15-mm Majorca and repeat the rest of the sequence in reverse. Set this strand (later referred to as "strand 1") aside.

2. String the following pearl sequence onto one spool of 32-gauge wire: Nine 4-mm buttons, one 7-mm Majorca, twenty 4-mm potatoes, one 7-mm Majorca, thirty-five 4-mm potatoes, one 7-mm Majorca, twenty 4-mm potatoes, one 7-mm Majorca, and nine 4-mm buttons. Set this strand (which will be referred to later as "strand 2") aside.

3. String one white stick pearl onto the remaining spool of 32-gauge wire. String on a sequence of one white stick and one gray potato four times. String on one stick, one diamond, and one stick. String on one gray potato and one white stick four times. String on one stick. Set it aside (it will subsequently be referred to it as "strand 3").

4. Make a slip knot at the end of strand 1, leaving a 3-inch (7.6 cm) tail. Slip the 5.5-mm hook inside the knot. Chain nine with wire only. Working with the strand's pearl sequence, make three chains that incorporate one pearl each. Chain eight with wire only.

5. Chain one, incorporating one pearl, and chain one with wire only. Repeat until you've used up all but three pearls. Chain eight. Make three chains that incorporate one pearl each. Chain nine and leave a 3-inch (7.6 cm) tail.

6. Use strand 2 to make a second row of crochet directly off of the crochet done with strand 1. Beginning on the inner end of strand 1 and leaving a 3-inch (7.6 cm) tail, use wire only to chain stitch until you reach the square pearl. Set down the hook.

7. Pull up one 4-mm potato until it's about ½ inch (1.3 cm) from the last chain. Fold the wire down around the pearl (figure 1). Grasp the pearl and wire tightly in your thumb and forefinger and make tight twists, creating a little pearl stem (figure 2). Repeat a few times in the same spot, varying the length of the stems to as long as ¾ inch (1.9 cm). Weave the wire end through the next chain and repeat across until you've used up all of the 4-mm potatoes and you reach the second square pearl.

fig. 1

fig. 2

8. Use the rest of strand 2 to chain across the rest of the same side of the necklace.

Tools

Flush cutters

Round-nose pliers

Crochet hook, 5.5 mm/U.S. 1

Crochet hook, 2.25 mm/U.S. 2

Crimping pliers (optional)

Techniques

Bead crochet (see sidebar on page 110)

Knotting (page 29)

9. Use strand 3 to repeat steps 6 and 7, but this time make the third row on the other side of strand 1, and space the twists evenly down the center of the necklace. Make the twists at least ¾ inch (1.9 cm) so the pearls dangle beneath the rest of the necklace.

10. Cut an 8-inch length of 28-gauge wire and weave it into the wires at one end of the necklace. *Note:* If the wires at the end of the necklace are unruly, attach the old wires to the new ones using crimp beads.

11. String on three 4-mm buttons and pass through the first hole of one half of the clasp two times. Pass through the second hole of the clasp from back to front. String on three 4-mm buttons and weave into the wires at the end of the necklace and back up. String on three 4-mm buttons and pass through the third hole of the clasp two times (figure 3). Secure the wire and trim. Repeat this step for the other end of the necklace.

fig. 3

Beaded Wire Crochet How-To

To begin beaded wire crochet, string beads onto a wire spool in the opposite order they'll be incorporated into the piece (the instructions on page 108 give the correct stringing order for this project). Let the beads fall next to the spool; don't cut the wire.

Form a loose slipknot at the end of the wire, leaving a 3-inch to 6-inch (7.6 cm to 15.2 cm) wire tail. Hold onto the tail as you place the crochet hook through the knot's loop and on top of the working wire (figure a). Bend the wire down over the side of the hook that's closest to you. Use the hook to catch the working wire as you pull it all the way through the first loop to make a second loop, or "chain stitch" (figure b).

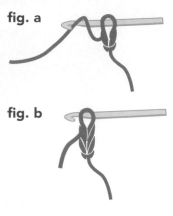

fig. a

fig. b

When you want to add a bead to the stitch, simply slide one down the wire until it hits the last chain stitch. Make another chain stitch as usual, allowing the bead to rest on one side of the work.

To work the second row of beaded wire crochet as in this project, start with a new length of beads strung onto spooled wire. Attach this new wire to the previous row by passing the hook through the first loop of the previous row and then making a chain stitch with the working wire (figure c). Continue across, making a line of stitches that are attached to the previous row. These subsequent stitches are also called "slip stitches."

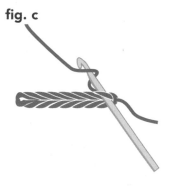

fig. c

Floating
Pearls

This very wearable design is as pretty as it is versatile.
Experiment with exchanging the pearl, wire, or chain type,
and you open up a world of possibilities.

Floating Pearls

Designer: Cynthia B. Wuller

Finished Size

15 inches (38.1 cm)

Materials

5 pink freshwater pearls, 4 x 5-mm teardrop

6 semiprecious rutilated quartz rounds, 3.5 mm

1 sterling silver hook-and-eye clasp, 20 mm

2 sterling silver jump rings, if needed to attach clasp

13-inch (33 cm) length of 1.5 mm sterling silver rollo chain

14¼-inch (36.2 cm) length of 22-gauge half-hard silver wire

Tools

Wire cutters

Ruler

2 chain-nose pliers

Round-nose pliers

Chasing hammer

Bench block

Bead reamer (optional)

Techniques

Wrapped loop (page 27)

Instructions

1. Cut three 2-inch (5.1 cm), two 2⅜-inch (6.1 cm), and one 3-inch (7.6 cm) pieces of wire. Cut two 6½-inch (16.5 cm) pieces of chain. Set aside.

2. Form a wrapped loop on one end of a 2-inch (5.1 cm) piece of wire. Slightly elongate the loop by using chain-nose pliers to carefully squeeze it (figure 1). Gently hammer the loop, avoiding the wrapped section. Hammer the straight wire for just a few taps to slightly flatten it. *Note:* The hammering on the straight portion is only to make the wire appear slimmer, so don't hammer too much or the pearl won't fit.

fig. 1

3. String one pearl on the wire. If the pearl doesn't fit, enlarge the hole with the bead reamer. Slide the pearl to the wrapped loop and hammer the tip of the wire on the bench block so the pearl can't slide off. Pull the pearl to the hammered tip. Use your fingers to gently bend a slight curve in the wire (figure 2).

fig. 2

4. Repeat steps 2 and 3 for the remaining 2-inch (5.1 cm) and 2⅜-inch (6.1 cm) wires so you have three short and two long dangles in all. Use chain-nose pliers to gently twist and adjust the dangles so each of the loops will face in the same direction when strung. Set aside.

5. Form one small wrapped loop on one end of the 3-inch (7.6 cm) wire that attaches to the end link of one of the chain lengths. On this wire, string on a sequence of one quartz round, one short dangle, one quartz round, and one long dangle. String on the same sequence again. Then string on one quartz round, one short dangle, and one quartz round. Form a wrapped loop on the open end of the wire that attaches to an end link on the other chain length. Use your thumb to gently curve the wire, taking care to keep it symmetrical (figure 3).

fig. 3

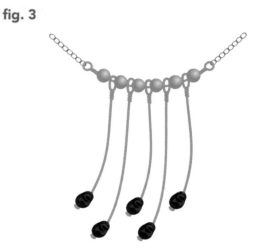

6. Attach one half of the clasp to the open link on one end of the chain. If needed, use a jump ring to do this. Repeat for the other half of the clasp at the other end of the chain.

Champagne
Bubbles

This needle-woven bracelet is easy to make once you get into the rhythm of the daisy chain pattern. Paired with the light-colored seed beads, the bright gold pearls seem to float around the wrist.

Finished Size

8¾ inches (22.2 cm)

Materials

21 bright gold crystal pearls, 6 mm

40 bright gold crystal pearls, 4 mm

Pearl-finish golden beige size 11° seed beads, 5 grams

12-foot (3.7 m) length of white or beige braided or nylon beading thread

Tools

Scissors

Beading needle, size 10

Techniques

Square knot (page 29)

Ladder stitch (page 30)

Simple fringe (page 30)

Instructions

Stitching the Bracelet

fig. 1

1. Cut 5 feet (1.5 m) of thread and pass it through the needle, leaving a 12-inch (30.5 cm) tail. String on 16 seed beads (beads 1-16). Use the tail and working thread to tie a square knot, forming a tight circle. Working in a clockwise direction, pass through all the beads again, exiting from bead 1 (figure 1).

fig. 2

2. String on one 6-mm pearl, and pass *back* through bead 9 so your needle goes in a counterclockwise direction. This seats the pearl in the center of the circle of beads (figure 2).

3. String on 15 seed beads, and pass through the bead you just exited. String on one 6-mm pearl and pass back through the eighth seed bead just strung.

fig. 3

4. Repeat step 3 until you've made 21 daisy chains or reach your desired bracelet length (figure 3).

5. Once you've added the last pearl, keep your needle moving in the same direction and weave through five more seed beads. Check to make sure there are no twists in your bracelet and that all the 6-mm pearls are on the same side of the bracelet.

6. String on one seed bead, one 4-mm pearl, and one seed bead. Pass through the third seed bead from the bead that connects the two daisies. Continue through the fourth and fifth seed beads. Repeat this step down the length of the bracelet (figure 4). When you come to the last daisy, weave through the seed beads to exit from the other side of the bracelet and repeat this step down the other side.

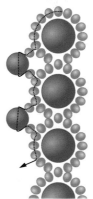

fig. 4

Adding the Clasp

7. Exit from one of the pairs of seed beads at the very end of the bracelet. String on two seed beads and pass through the two seed beads at the end of the bracelet. Pass through the two seed beads just added once more. Continue working a two-bead-high ladder stitch for four stitches (figure 5).

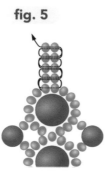

fig. 5

8. String on 14 seed beads and pass through the last ladder stitch again to make a loop. Weave through the beads and exit from the third bead added in this step.

9. String on one 6-mm pearl and pass through the seed bead directly opposite the one you last exited to seat the pearl. *Note:* Check to be sure this pearl sits on the same side of the bracelet as the other 6-mm pearls. Continue weaving through the loop's seed beads, exiting at the same point you added the 6-mm pearl in this step. Pass through the pearl again.

10. String on one 4-mm pearl and one seed bead. Pass back through the pearl to make a fringe leg. Pass back through the 6-mm pearl. Repeat this step to create another fringe leg at the other side of the 6-mm pearl. Exit from the first 4-mm pearl placed with the needle pointing toward the 6-mm pearl (figure 6).

fig. 6

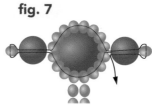

11. Weave through the seed beads of the loop until you reach the opposite 4-mm pearl. Pass through it, the fringe leg's end seed bead, and back through the pearl. Pass through the rest of the loop's seed beads (figure 7). Repeat the thread path once to secure the fringe legs to the loop, finishing the toggle bar.

fig. 7

12. Pass through all the beads that make up the toggle bar several times to reinforce. Weave through the ladder-stitched beads to reinforce. Secure the thread in the body of the bracelet and trim.

13. Thread the needle with the tail thread. Repeat step 8, this time making three two-bead-high ladder stitches.

14. String on 18 seed beads and pass through the last ladder stitch again to make a loop. Pass through all these beads again to reinforce the loop. Weave through the ladder-stitched beads to reinforce. Secure the thread in the body of the bracelet and trim.

Star Flowers

The design of this ornate necklace pairs needle-and-thread techniques with wireworked ones. The result is an Art Nouveau–inspired piece that features a variety of pearls.

Star Flowers

Designer: Jean Campbell

Finished Size

17 inches (43.2 cm)

Materials

40 peridot freshwater pearls, 6-mm button

20 ivory freshwater pearls, 6-mm
top-drilled potato

1 ivory freshwater pearl, 6-mm
center-drilled potato

6 ivory crystal pearls, 6 x 12-mm vertically-
drilled teardrop

2 dark olive crystal pearl rounds, 12 mm

2 dark olive crystal pearl rounds, 8 mm

7 dark olive crystal pearl rounds, 6 mm

10 iridescent smoke crystal bicones, 6 mm

30 iridescent smoke crystal bicones, 4 mm

10 sterling silver seamless rounds, 3 mm

22 sterling silver seamless rounds, 2 mm

5 grams of metallic silver charlottes

1 sterling silver 22-gauge head pin, 1 inch
(2.5 cm) long

10 sterling silver 22-gauge eye pins,
1½ inches (3.8 cm) long

10 sterling silver 2.5-mm jump rings

1 sterling silver fish hook clasp, 18 mm

8-inch (20.3 cm) length of sterling silver fig-
ure-eight chain (large links are 6 x 10 mm)

Moss-colored 6-pound braided
beading thread

Watchmaker's glue (optional)

Instructions

Preparing the Chain and Beaded Links

1. Cut five pieces of chain, one that includes five large chain links (2½ inches [6.3 cm]); and four that include two large chain links (⅞ inch [2.2 cm]). Set the long chain and the short chains aside.

2. Slide a 6-mm crystal round onto the head pin. Make a wrapped loop that attaches to one end of the longest chain length. Set aside.

3. Slip a 6-mm crystal round onto an eye pin. Make a simple loop to secure the bead and trim the excess wire. Repeat to make six 6-mm beaded links in all. Set aside.

4. Slide an 8-mm crystal round onto an eye pin. Make a simple loop to secure the bead and trim the excess wire. Repeat to make a second 8-mm beaded link. Set aside.

5. Slip a 12-mm crystal round onto an eye pin. Make a simple loop to secure the bead and trim the excess wire. Repeat to make one more 12-mm beaded link. Set aside.

Stitching the Small Flower Links

6. Cut a 3-foot (91.4 cm) length of thread and thread the needle. String on five button pearls, leaving a 4-inch (10.2 cm) tail. Use a square knot to tie the pearls into a tight foundation circle. Pass through the first pearl strung.

7. String on one 4-mm bicone and one charlotte. Pass back through the bicone and through the next pearl of the foundation circle to make a fringe leg. Repeat this step around the circle to add five bicone fringe legs (or "petals") in all.

8. String on one charlotte and pass through the next pearl of the foundation circle (figure 1). Repeat around to add five charlottes in all. *Note:* Be sure that the charlottes are placed so they sit on the same side of each bicone in order to end up with a flower "front." Weave through all the beads of the flower to reinforce. Use a thread burner to trim the thread close to the work. Set aside.

fig. 1

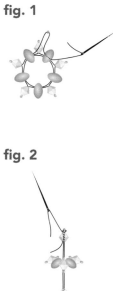

fig. 2

6. Thread the needle with an 8-inch (20.3 cm) length of thread. String on one 4-mm bicone and one charlotte, leaving a 2-inch (5.1 cm) tail. Pass back through the bicone and tie a square knot close to the beads. Pass through the flower created in steps 6 to 8. String on one 4-mm bicone and one charlotte. Pass back through the bicone just strung and through the bicone and charlotte previously strung in this step (figure 2). Pass back and forth through all these beads to secure and tighten the beaded flower. Secure the thread and use a thread burner to trim the thread close to the work. Set aside.

7. Repeat steps 6 through 9 to make four small flower links in all.

Tools

Wire cutters

Chain-nose pliers

Round-nose pliers

Scissors

English beading needle, size 12

Thread burner

Techniques

Wrapped loop (page 27)

Simple loop (page 26)

Knotting (page 29)

Simple fringe (page 30)

Stitching the Medium Flower Links

11. Follow steps 6 to 8, this time using top-drilled 6-mm pearls for the petals in step 7.

12. Cut an 8-inch (20.3 cm) piece of thread and thread the needle. String on one 4-mm bicone and one charlotte, leaving a 2-inch (5.1 cm) tail. Pass back through the bicone and tie a square knot close to the beads. Pass through the flower created in step 11. Sew down through one side of the figure eight on a short chain and up through the other side of the figure eight (figure 3). Pass back up through the bicone and charlotte just strung and back down through the bicone. Pass back and forth through the beads and chain to secure and tighten the flower to the chain. Use a thread burner to trim the thread close to the work. Set aside.

fig. 3

13. Repeat steps 11 and 12 to make another medium flower link.

Stitching the Center Flower

14. Thread the needle with a 3-foot (91.4 cm) length of thread. String on ten button pearls, leaving a 4-inch (10.2 cm) tail. Use a square knot to tie the pearls into a tight foundation circle. Pass through the first pearl strung.

15. String on one 6-mm bicone and one charlotte. Pass back through the bicone and through the next button pearl of the foundation circle. String on one 10-mm teardrop pearl and one charlotte. Pass back through the teardrop pearl and through the next button pearl of the foundation circle. Repeat this step around the circle to add five bicones and five teardrop pearl petals in all (figure 4).

fig. 4

16. String on one 2-mm round and pass through the next pearl of the foundation circle. String on one 3-mm round and pass through the next pearl of the foundation circle. Repeat around to add five 2-mm and five 3-mm rounds in all. *Note:* Be sure that the beads are placed so they sit on the same side of each petal bead, the 2-mm rounds over the bicones of the previous step and the 3-mm rounds over the pearls of the previous step. Exit from the first bead added in this step.

17. String on one 6-mm top-drilled pearl and pass through the next round from the previous step. Repeat around to add ten top-drilled pearls in all. Exit from the first bead added in this step.

18. String on one 2-mm round and pass through the next top-drilled pearl added in the previous step. Repeat around to add ten 2-mm rounds in all. Exit from a 2-mm round added in this step that sits over a 6-mm bicone added in step 15.

19. String on one 6-mm bicone and one 2-mm round. Pass back through the bicone. Pass through the 2-mm round last exited so the thread passes through in the same direction as you exited it. Pass through the next top-drilled pearl (added in step 17), the following 2-mm round added in the previous step, the next top-drilled pearl, and the following 2-mm round added in the previous step (figure 5). Repeat around to add five 6-mm bicone fringe legs in all.

fig. 5

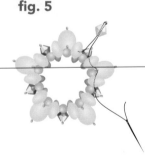

20. Weave the thread up through one of the 6-mm bicone fringe legs to exit from a 2-mm round. Pass through the 2-mm round at the end of the adjacent fringe leg. Repeat around to connect the fringe legs, pulling the

2-mm rounds into a tight circle (figure 6). Weave through all the beads of the flower to reinforce. Use a thread burner to trim the thread close to the work. Set aside.

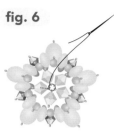

fig. 6

21. Cut an 8-inch (20.3 cm) length of thread and thread the needle. String on one 10-mm teardrop pearl and one 2-mm round, leaving a 2-inch (5.1 cm) tail. Pass back through the teardrop pearl and tie a square knot close to the beads. Pass up through the flower center (from the back to the front). String on one center-drilled 6-mm pearl and one 2-mm round. Pass back through the pearl and the rest of the beads previously strung in this step. Pass back and forth through all these beads to secure and tighten the flower. Secure the thread and use a thread burner to trim the thread close to the work. Set aside.

Assembling the Necklace

22. Attach a jump ring to the charlotte at the end of a petal on one of the small flowers. Skip one fringe leg and add another jump ring in the same manner. Repeat for all the small flowers and the center flower. Set aside.

23. In series, connect the necklace components as follows: The clasp; one 6-mm beaded link; one short chain; one 6-mm beaded link; one small flower (using the attached jump rings); one 6-mm beaded link; one small flower; one 8-mm beaded link; one medium flower; and one 12-mm beaded link. Connect the center flower.

24. Repeat step 23 in reverse, ending the sequence with the long chain instead of the clasp.

25. If necessary to keep the petals of the centerpiece and medium flowers in place, dab a very small amount of glue at the connection between the button and top-drilled pearls.

Mirtha Aertker is a native of Venezuela who has lived all over the world. She is a potter and mixed-media artist who gained a true passion for jewelry making when she moved to Dallas, Texas, where she now resides. In 2003 Mirtha was awarded third place in a national competition for silversmiths in Lima, Peru, and her work has been included in many art events, including the Pink Pearl. Contact Mirtha at mirtha. aertker@gmail.com. Her website address is www. clayniche.com.

Sharon Bateman is a mixed-media artist best known for her many magazine articles, appearances on DIY's *Jewelry Making* show, and beading books, including her self-published titles *Morning Rose Rosette, Peepers and Creepers,* and *Over the Edge.* She invented and manufactures Sharondipity Tube Looms, which are clear plastic looms designed for specific projects. Contact Sharon at www.sharonbateman.com.

Lisa M. Call is a jewelry designer who has been creating and crafting in an array of mediums all her life. She left the corporate world to raise her daughters and find time for other interests. Wirework, metal, and beads are her main passions, and she has spent the last five years focusing on metalsmithing, wireworking, and beading. Lisa is also a certified Precious Metal Clay artisan. Contact her at www.lisamariecall.com.

Jean Campbell is a freelance editor and writer whose specialty is beading. She is the founding editor of *Beadwork* magazine and has written and edited more than 30 books, including the recent titles *The Art of Beaded Beads* (2006) and *Beading with Crystals* (2007), both published by Lark Books. She has appeared on the DIY *Jewelry Making* show, *The Shay Pendray Show,* and PBS' *Beads, Baubles, and Jewels.* Jean lives with her family in Minneapolis.

Marie Lee Carter began learning her craft in classes at the Fashion Institute of Technology, the Brookfield Craft Center, and the 92nd Street Y. She has focused on developing skills that express emotions through shape and color. With each design, Marie aims to tell a short story in metal and stone. She lives with her husband and son in New York. Contact her at www.mariecarter.com.

Pat Evans is a mixed-media artist who lives in San Jose, California. She enjoys learning, teaching, and writing about new techniques in the jewelry, glass, fiber, and paper arts and is a certified instructor for both Precious Metal Clay and Art Clay. A recently-retired elementary school teacher and the mother of five adult children, Pat especially enjoys helping young and young-at-heart students to discover their innate creative abilities. Email her at pat@patevansdesigns.com.

Nadine Fidelman discovered her hidden talent as a wireworker after leaving the teaching profession eight years ago. Since then, her desire to create beautiful pieces of gemstone, fossil, pearl, and dichroic-glass jewelry fills her time. Nadine is a certified instructor for Precious Metal Clay and has taught several classes in wire jewelry-making techniques. She sells her work at many craft shows and at the Kress Emporium in Asheville, North Carolina. Nadine lives in the Asheville area with her husband, son, and two standard poodles. Her website is www.jewelrybynadine.com.

Ellen Gerritse is a world traveler who currently lives in Kuwait. She works primarily as a silversmith and has taught fine arts in Europe and Asia. Ellen finds herself drawn to create objects from simple, accessible materials with the few tools she has close at hand, and she loves to combine her metalwork with other materials, including papier-mâché. In 2006 she won the Collectors' Choice Award during the Mind Over Metal show in Houston, Texas.

Elizabeth Larsen works as a biologist but started beading as a hobby to challenge her creative side. Elizabeth began making jewelry in 2001 after taking a class in chain making at a local bead store. She uses this technique as a base to create bold yet feminine pieces of art jewelry. Elizabeth lives in Snohomish, Washington, with her husband, Mitch; stepson, Nico; and their three dogs, Misha, Rocky, and Cordelia. Contact her at elarsen2003@yahoo.com.

Janet A. Lasher has been creating embellished textiles, beadwork, and other wearable art forms since she was old enough to sit in front of a sewing machine. For 25 years she had a career as a corporate analyst while at the same time creating award-winning, wearable art garments. In 2004 she left her corporate position in order to focus on developing more complicated fiber sculptures. Her work is found in private and corporate collections, including the Bernina International Collection in Switzerland. Janet works in her studio, teaches embellishment and surface design, and lives with her husband and teenage son in Charlotte, North Carolina.

Diana Light is an artist who lives in the mountains of Western North Carolina, where she creates beauty out of anything she gets her hands on. She's especially attracted to shiny objects and believes a girl can never have too much bling. Diana holds a bachelor of fine arts degree in painting and printmaking from the University of North Carolina Greensboro.

Sandra Lupo has been making jewelry for 20 years and continues to be amazed at the myriad of pearl shapes, colors, and design possibilities. She is a regular contributor to Lark Books and *Step-by-Step Beads* magazine and has designed kits for Touchstone Crystal. Sandra has taught jewelry-making classes at the Swarovski Create-Your-Style Show in Tucson, Beadfest, Jewelry Arts Expo Wirefest, and the Newark Museum Arts Workshop. Contact her at sandra@sandsstones.com.

Andrea L. McLester worked for 10 years as a theatrical designer, creating designs for some of the world's leading dance and opera companies and a television network. Andrea also worked as a costumer, designing jewelry and fabrics for legendary stage performers. After an injury cut short her career in show business, Andrea convalesced by learning basic metalsmithing skills and developed a deep love of glass. In 2003 she created a one-of-a-kind necklace for Saks Fifth Avenue's Key to the Cure, a national fundraising event chaired by actress Nicole Kidman. Andrea's work has been featured in *Creative Silver Chains* (2005) and *Contemporary Bead and Wire Jewelry* (2006), both published by Lark Books. Andrea lives in the Washington, D.C. area.

Nathalie Mornu works as an editor at Lark Books. Occasionally getting the opportunity to design projects for books gives her a chance to dabble at various crafts. Her projects appear in, among other Lark Books titles, *Decorating Your First Apartment* (2003), *Making Gingerbread Houses* (2004), *Creative Stitching on Paper* (2006), and *Pretty Little Pincushions* (2007). She is the co-author of *Contemporary Bead & Wire Jewelry* (2006) and *Survival Sewing* (2007) and the author of *Cutting-Edge Decoupage* (2007), all Lark Books titles. She is currently obsessed with embroidery.

Jean Power is a beader, jewelry maker, writer, and teacher who lives and works in London, England. She loves all aspects of beading and jewelry making, from beading and bead embroidery to wirework and chain mail. As well as having her work published in a variety of magazines, she has co-authored two beading books and is the editor of *Bead*, the United Kingdom's only beading and jewelry magazine. Contact Jean at www.jeanpower.com.

Debra Saldivar grew up in a family of artists but didn't think she'd received her parents' creative genes until she was in her thirties. Since that time, her skills have evolved to include jewelry making and metalwork. Debra owns Luna Azul Designs in Port Orchard, Washington, where she sells jewelry-making supplies and teaches classes, providing a place for people to relax, learn, and be inspired. Debra lives on the Kitsap Peninsula in Washington and can be contacted at www.lunaazuldesigns.com.

Katherine Song holds a master's degree in fashion design from the Northwest Institute of Textile and Technology in Xian, China. In 2000 she moved to Toronto, Canada, and worked as a designer for John Bead Corp. Ltd. Her work is featured in *Beading with Crystals* (Lark Books, 2007). Katherine launched her own Toronto-based jewelry business, Katherine Song Designs, in 2007. She may be contacted at www.katherinesong.com.

Cynthia Wuller is a jewelry maker whose work is largely inspired by female figures in fairy tales, folklore, and mythology. She strives for her designs to have a delicate, feminine look, yet to be tough and durable when handled—much like the heroines in fables. Cynthia holds a bachelor of fine arts degree from the School of the Art Institute of Chicago, with a background in fashion, fiber, and metalworking. Her work has appeared in *The Art of Jewelry: Paper Jewelry* (2006) and will appear in *The Art of Jewelry: Wood* (2008), both published by Lark Books. Contact Cynthia at cbwuller@yahoo.com.

Nancy Zellers started working with beads full time in the late 1990s. Her work has been featured in many magazines, including *Beadwork, Step-by-Step Beads,* and *Bead & Button*. She also has work featured in many books, including *500 Beaded Objects* (2004), *The Art of Beaded Beads* (2006), and *Beading with Crystals* (2007), all published by Lark Books. Her sculptural pieces have appeared in several contemporary art shows regionally and nationally, and she is a sought-after beadwork instructor. Contact Nancy at www.nzbeads.com.

Acknowledgments

Thank you to Chevron Trading Post & Bead Co., which loaned many of the findings and materials pictured in the front sections of the book. Not only does this shop carry a beautiful assortment of pearls, it also has an amazingly huge selection of all types of beads. If you're crazy about beading, check out Chevron if you're ever in downtown Asheville, North Carolina.

Pearls are notoriously difficult to photograph. Stewart O'Shields shot images that make the projects sing.

J'aime Allene and Bonnie Brooks contributed their extraordinary skills as both artists and beaders to render all the how-to illustrations in this book. Their careful drawings will help projects stay on track.

The editorial department is fortunate to have the eagle eyes of Julie Hale and Matt Paden. We're grateful for their careful attention to detail. Thanks also to the art department assistants—Jeff Hamilton and Avery Johnson—for their unwavering support during the book's production process.

Most importantly, this book wouldn't exist without the talented designers who shared their passion for pearls. Thank you all for being a part of this project.

Index